THORNABY
LIVES

Derek Smith

1892 -1992

Previous page: Thornaby's main meeting place, The Five Lamps looking towards Acklam Road in about 1910.

INTRODUCTION

This is a people's account of an eventful century from 1892 when Thornaby became a Borough by Royal charter, across industrial peaks and troughs to Mrs Thatcher's iconic "Walk in the wilderness" which for many represented the passing of Britain's industrial age. Thornaby was certainly a town of toil, people were drawn here during the 19th century in their thousands to work in the emerging industries from all parts of the United Kingdom and their jobs were often arduous with 50 hour weeks being common. A working life could begin in childhood at 13 years and until long after the NHS arrived many industrial workers never lived to reach the age of 65 year to collect their pensions. Yet many of the products Thornaby people made have survived, the identifying plaques may have gone but the bridges, dock installations and pipework made in the town are there still doing their jobs around the world today.

Over 75 people have been interviewed for their stories and photographs and searches made in the archives of more to try to capture some of the spirit of a close knit community, especially the sense of togetherness and pride. Sadly, over the years many working people lived and died here without there being very much evidence of their existence. Testimonies and personal photographs are essential to capturing what a place and it's people were like because once beyond living memory communities easily disappear. There is very little documented for example of the workers who constructed the 900 ships built at Teesdale, Thornaby's industrial hub where they made an incredible contribution to the local and national economy, the 1980's development of the site included no sign or monument to acknowledge any of this remarkable history.

This book tries to address these gaps with the help of residents, local libraries, archives, and newspapers, together with my own collection of photographs. Most valuable has been the Remembering Thornaby Group archive gathered by enthusiasts across 25 years between 1990 and 2015. This book shows that everyone has interesting stories to tell us, often with photographs to illustrate them. We hope that present and future generations will be able to learn from Thornaby's rich past and as the field work continues more material will surface to develop oral history further so that Thornaby's hard working people can continue to be both remembered and celebrated.

Great Public Rejoicing: Thornaby is Created.

The development of Thornaby had been remarkable, no more than 160 people were to be found in Thornaby village in 1811, the sole community and where the population had remained steady for more than 200 years. By 1861, 3130 people lived in nearby South Stockton and by 1892 the town population had grown to 15,600 and it continued to expand. People from all over the United Kingdom seeking a better life came to Thornaby to work in the emerging industries, from rural poverty, famine in Ireland, from other industrial towns and they brought their skills with them. On 6th October 1892 The Municipal town of Thornaby was created from the Local Board of South Stockton the community that had grown around the industrial hub of Teesdale and the Village. 18 months earlier 80% of the residents signed a petition requesting the creation of a municipal borough and the Act of Parliament was the result. Workers were given a holiday on Charter Day and there was great public rejoicing. The municipal buildings on Mandale Road were thronged with thousands of spectators and the Charter was read out on the Town Hall balcony by the incoming MP. Sir Thomas Wrightson and he proposed that the assembled Burgesses and inhabitants accept it. Feasts for 200 aged poor of goose, duck, roast beef and plum puddings and teas for schoolchildren were laid on. Music from Whitwell's brass band played to the crowds gathered at Thornaby Racecourse where the day culminated in a grand firework display.

A pre-restoration photograph of the clock which was started on 27th January 1892 and along with works hooters helped to regulate the lives of citizens within hearing distance chiming at each quarter and at each hour.

The Macebearer William Callendar leads the annual procession from the Town Hall on Mayor's Day 1937. Mayor Harold Dacre with the Town Clerk J.R. Carr, and the head of the Catholic community Father George Kiernan on a day of great civic pride.

Now this town has come into the category of municipal boroughs it will be governed by the popular vote, governed by those who are sent there by the will of the people to conduct all the affairs according to their will and for their benefit.
Cleveland MP Henry Fell Pease at the inauguration ceremony.

The massive expansion of urban population during the mid 19th century led to great concern over public health and poverty and who should be best responsible for their treatment. Threats such as cholera for example were ever present in expanding communities that were unplanned and built by unregulated private developers. A governmental body responsible for administrating public health, and the poor law was clearly needed. The 1892 creation of Thornaby followed the Local government act of 1888 which introduced a standardised system of local government with the legal responsibility for carrying out these important duties. One of the first jobs at Thornaby not surprisingly was to appoint a Public Health Officer. Committees were formed to deal with a range of key areas such as sanitation so that important water, drainage and sewage infrastructure could be installed and maintained. The public library, cemetery, public housing, police and fire brigade were all now responsibilities of Thornaby Town Council. The Council performed it's duties admirably for 76 years until 1968 when the Thornaby Town Council lost it's autonomy and became part of the larger Borough of Teesside.

The Council Chamber in 1900, the centre piece of an architecturally impressive building constructed between 1890 and 1892 and designed by James Garry of West Hartlepool.

Essential services such as the police force and fire brigade were civic responsibilities. The 1903 brigade display their steam water pump and escape chute at the Chapel Street station. Bearded right is fire chief Captain J.R. Tranter. The station moved to George Street soon after and was until 1972 a retained brigade of volunteer firemen.

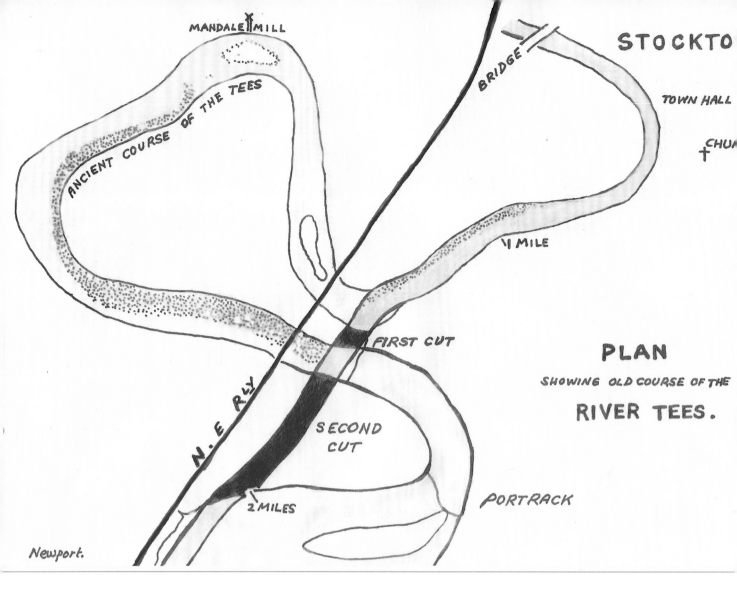

Two Cuts

Industrial Thornaby would probably never have developed without two cuts made across the course of the river Tees at Mandale and Portrack which vastly improved navigation. In 1791 work began on the 220 yard Mandale Cut which took ten years to complete. Then in 1810 work started on the second Portrack Cut of 770 yards which opened in 1831. Sections of the old river can still be found on edges of Teesside Park retail, previously Stockton Racecourse. Life and work on the river expanded dramatically during the 19th century and by 1892 Thornaby was thriving with a range of industries. Until the early 19th century ships often took days to navigate the Tees as far as Stockton. Sandbanks and the winding course made it an ordeal until the lengthy excavations which involved hundreds of men in years of digging. The two cuts reduced the journey time to hours and raised the level of the river enabling larger beamed ships to berth. This brilliant piece of engineering was responsible for bringing work to Thornaby and Stockton. As a result of the transformation Thornaby was able to support two major shipyards, Richardson Duck and Craig Taylor. Producers relied on shipping and well maintained berths to import their raw materials then export their goods, the Tees Conservancy Commission ensured the river was clear through regular dredging.

The river was an important part of life in Thornaby whether for pleasure or work. 1948 and a team of cleaners is being rowed to a ship by Jimmy Kelly whose family worked the ferry between Portrack and Teesdale for three generations. The cleaners include Elsie Scholes, Ginny Allison, Dolly Skellet and Rosie Snow.

A dredger clears the mud banks near Craig Taylor's yard before a launch for the Tees Conservancy Commission who maintained the busy river.

I served my time as a boat builder at Richard Pickersgill in 1936 and built my first boat at 17. We built lifeboats, cobbles and motor launches based on two types, "Clinker" and "Carvell" Everything was made by hand but we had electric saws for heavy cutting. We used adges, draw knives and wooden planes on mainly English and Japanese oak, the seats were redwood and the gunwhales elm and oak. The leading hand fixed the first six frames then we would follow on. Working on piecework a boat could be finished in ten days. The boatyard closed after the war. MATTHEW MARLEY

Mr Davies , right, of Davies boatyard later Pickersgills with his new motor launch under Victoria Bridge in about 1920. In the distance, the busy Cleveland Flour Mill wharves. Above, a crew finish off a motor launch about 1930.

We used dad's rowing boat for a family day out. The Tees was a fast flowing river so you tried to time the boat on a Sunday morning when the tide was going up the river. There was my gran, my grand dad, my uncles, everybody, 15 or 16 of us going up towards Preston Park and Yarm. Then we all piled out on the riverbank and we used a primus stove to put the kettle on and have a picnic. We'd stop up and when the tide changed we all came back down with the tide. It wasn't as polluted in them days there was a lot of fish. When the tide went out there'd be flatties and sea trout on the river bank, as kids you'd pick them up in your hands and they'd be flapping, still alive. JACK GREEN

The iconic flour mill dominates this 1950's scene. On the right in front of the bridge, the site of Pickersgill's boat yard. The Cake Mill and Manure works were located between the Flour mill and the bridge, in this picture they are long gone and their wharves derelict.

Cleveland Flour mill workers on their break about 1950, foreground in hat Jack Humphries and son Fred far right

Thornaby riverside was busy with ships thanks to well constructed wharfs and Tees Conservancy Commission dredging to keep the riverbanks clear for ships to dock. Many firms had their own extensive quays. By Victoria Bridge three Mills, each important employers, were close neighbours with contrasting products. The Cleveland Flour Mill opened in 1871 with impressive north and south buildings that became Teesside landmarks, at it's peak it employed 200 people. With extensive machinery the mill produced 5000 sacks of flour a week at one point but in spite of major investment made little profit until the 1930's. The Mill had it's own fleet of cargo ships and in 1894 a new wharf was installed .

The new equipment involved the trunk of an elevator tower built on the wharf connecting straight to the docked ship hold to import 30 tons of grain an hour into the silos. However profits were affected by the fluctuating price of flour and wheat and wheat was often imported from India and the USA. In 1893 for example a small profit was typically recorded, in 1897 a major loss for the whole company forced it into receivership and it was up for auction. A succession of new owners failed to turn round the Mill to make a profit and it was finally taken over by Joseph Rank in 1928. In 1954 there was a major fire which extensively damaged the warehouses, it appears to have closed in about 1960. The Cleveland Flour Mill remained derelict until demolition in 1970.

The impressive ferro-concrete silo replaced the old north tower which was demolished in 1911. In 1970 the mill was demolished and became a local spectacle taking four days to bring down completely using 256 lbs of gelignite.

Tees from Victoria Bridge, Stockton-on-Tees.

North of England Pure Oil and Cake co began in 1869 on a half acre site sandwiched between the flour mill and the Bone Mill. They had large seed chambers of linseed and 700 tons of cottonseed, the oilhouse had 13 tanks. Their most popular product was their N.E.P Feeding cakes for cattle. The mill finished in 1913 and the Cleveland flour mill moved onto the site as part of the North tower development.

The Tees Bone Mill was set up in 1863 to manufacture fertilisers and manure, it's products were excellent and in demand from farmers, however the process was notorious for emitting terrible smells. Raw materials included crushed bone and guano imported from South America, there was also much bone boiling. The Council Sanitary Committee moved to take legal proceedings against the mill several times. As a result the company reinvented itself changing it's name to the Tees Refining Company in 1910 and seems to have reduced it's emissions but closed in 1923.

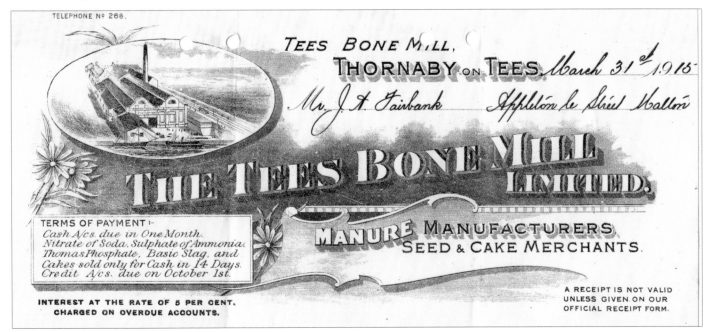

Shipyards

Britain was a supreme leader in shipbuilding, between 1890 and 1914 producing 60% of the world's stock, the two shipyards at Thornaby made a significant contribution, building ships for a range of clients around the world as well as for the UK. Richardson Duck began in 1854 and Craig Taylor in 1884 and made first class cargo and oil steamers, passenger ships and lighters. Although the size and depth of the river Tees at Thornaby limited the ships the yards could make, they took advantage of the worldwide demand for tramp steamers which were an average of 300 ft long. The yards were innovative, Craig Taylor for example built some of the first all steel ships and ingeniously in the 1890's moved into the relatively new field of oil tankers and built vessels that could be converted to carry ordinary cargo should there be a dip in trade. At their peak these two shipyards employed nearly 1600 people.

You'd see a sea of faces coming up Trafalgar Street, you can imagine 1,250 men, something like that. It was absolutely crowded with work people. But it was the gateway to a lot of works down there when Head Wrightson's were working as well as the shipyards, Craig Taylors and Richardson and Duck's. And there was Whitwell's Iron Foundry, Crosthwaite's Iron Foundry, all down Trafalgar Street, and it was a hive of activity.
MAYNARD WILSON

Top: a crowd at Stockton quayside watch the launch of the iron screw cargo ship Rosecliffe from Craig Taylor's yard in July 1888.

Right: primitive scaffolding made from wood piles driven into the riverbank mud led to many accidents. The 305 foot steel screw steamer Kildare being prepared for launching In September 1903.

This group of workmen with their foreman in the early 1900's may be selected invitees to an official ship handover party. On the stocks behind them is the frame of another ship in progress.

The two yards built over 900 vessels between them, but at great human cost. Thirty men were killed in the two yards over the years and many more injured. The primitive scaffolding used had barely changed since Henry the Eighth built his navy. Men frequently fell from platforms and heavy tools were often accidentally dropped on to men working below.

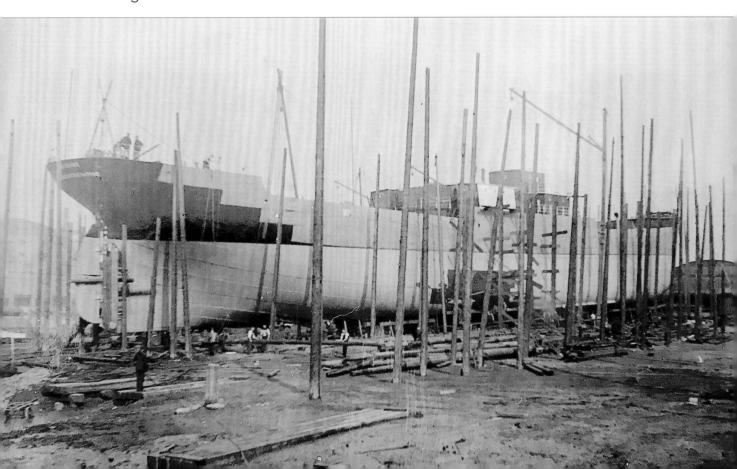

Above: The nearly completed shell of an unidentified ship ready for cladding.
The boy riveter could be as young as thirteen, which is when work began for many in
Thornaby at the beginning of the 20th Century.

George Butt Craig, senior partner at the
Craig Taylor yard brought his considerable
skills to Thornaby after training on
Clydeside. He was Mayor of the town and
gifted a Mayorial chain in 1904 to
commemorate his three years in the post.

Built in 1900 the offices of Craig Taylor with their
distinctive cupolas. They were taken over by
Head Wrightson when the company closed

Right, a work party, Craig Taylor about 1910.

International trade: sea trials for The Acre completed in July 1906, a 2587 ton steel screw steamer for Lloyd Brazileiro a Brazilian company, the cargo ship was in service until 1961. The Acre also had passenger cabins and the steamship company based in Rio de Janeiro advertised passages along the North Brazilian coast with "superior passenger accommodation" Some of the party on deck could well be from Rio and may have returned with the ship to Brazil after trials.

Bottom of picture on left: the two Thornaby yards during the early 1920's, Richardson Duck left of Trafalgar Street which runs at 45 degrees and Craig Taylor on the right. Across the river bottom left on the North Shore is Ropners shipyard. In ten years all the berths in this view will be derelict.

Kingfield a cargo ship built by Richardson Duck in 1902. The Kingfield finished service in the USSR in 1960.

The Rosemary a frigate for the Admiralty completed by Richardson Duck in December 1915 ready for war service.

The Conistone the penultimate ship built at Richardson Duck completed in May 1924.

Left, The Svaland built as Scottish Moors at Richardson Duck in 1890.

Building a Town

Thornaby extended substantially beyond Teesdale and the railway line from the 1860's. Architects were rarely involved in domestic housing, instead builders worked from catalogues of standard designs. Industrial dwellings were simple with minimal ornament, terraces were usually two up and two down. Most importantly there was access to clean water in most of the post 1870 homes in Thornaby ensured by a Water Board set up in 1876 to build reservoirs after the local cholera epidemics of the 1850's. Gas was available but more common by the turn of the century, instead coal fuelled cast iron kitchen ranges offered facilities for cooking and drying clothes. Some residents, like those in Barnard Street overleaf would have to wait until 1954 for electrification.

Right, 1890's development by Sedgwick Brothers

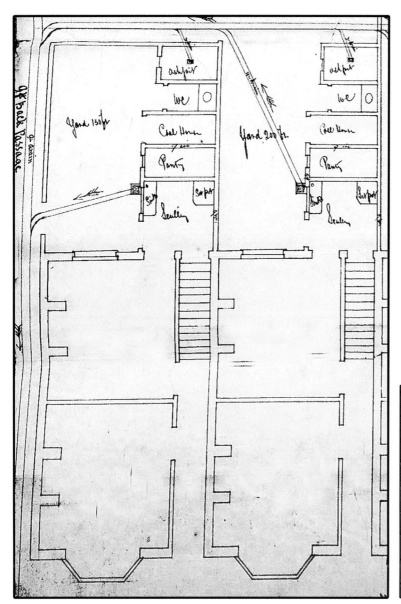

Plan for two houses in Barnard Street 1871.
Below Howard Fulton leaves a house in the same row a hundred years later in 1971 before demolition for the A66 carriageway. Howard had lived in the 11 Barnard Street since 1912. The terrace was slightly superior to the homes opposite having a bay window and three bedrooms. Water closets were introduced just before the second world war before then ash pits were used and the human waste gathered by council night soil scavengers, below, ash pit door in back lane.

Right, St. Luke's church under construction 1906.

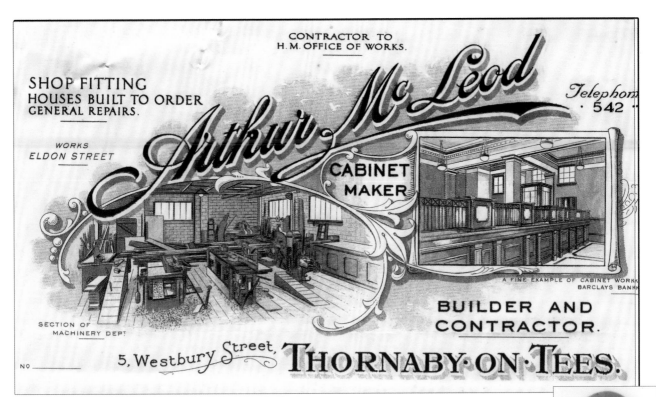

CONTRACTOR TO
H.M. OFFICE OF WORKS.

SHOP FITTING
HOUSES BUILT TO ORDER
GENERAL REPAIRS.

Arthur McLeod

Telephone
· 542 ·

CABINET
MAKER

WORKS
ELDON STREET

A FINE EXAMPLE OF CABINET WORK
BARCLAYS BANK

SECTION OF
MACHINERY DEP?

BUILDER AND
CONTRACTOR.

5, Westbury Street, THORNABY·ON·TEES.

N°

Thornaby expanded dramatically and there was a good supply of skilled local builders to meet the increasing demand for property. Arthur McLeod, active from the end of the 19th century was one. Based in Westbury Street McLeod performed a range of work including cabinet making for commercial interiors. His company built the Globe Theatre completed in 1936 in Stockton. Right, a dream home on Thornaby Road.

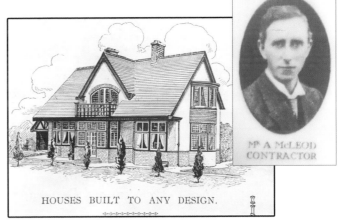

HOUSES BUILT TO ANY DESIGN.

M? A McLEOD
CONTRACTOR

WORKMEN AND STAFF OF CHAS.P. KINNELL. LTD., VULCAN IRON W

A Foundry Town

The construction boom at the end of the 19th Century and Edwardian Britain created a huge demand for ironwork especially drainage and gas pipes for homes. With plenty of raw materials nearby and good access to rail, the conditions for foundry production were ideal at Thornaby and soon it had eight busy establishments. The foundry fumes caused respiratory problems for some of the long term workers and pneumoconiosis was common. But moulders enjoyed their jobs even though the peaks and troughs of market demand could involve short term working and less pay some weeks.

Taken in 1908 not long after Charles P. Kinnell's Vulcan Ironworks was established in 1899 on the riverside site of the Tees Bottling Company. This light foundry made cast iron piping for central heating systems, soil pipes and gas and water mains and continued into the 1950's.

S, THORNABY ON TEES.

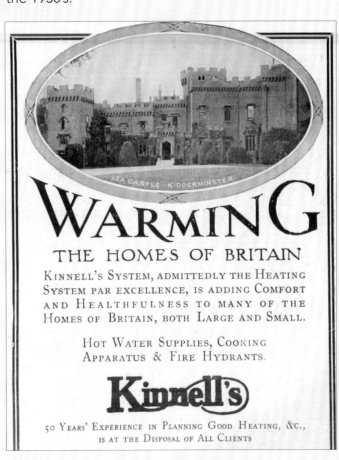

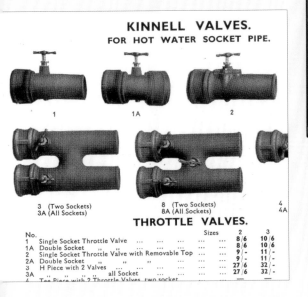

KINNELL VALVES.
FOR HOT WATER SOCKET PIPE.

1   1A   2

3 (Two Sockets)   8 (Two Sockets)   4
3A (All Sockets)   8A (All Sockets)   4A

THROTTLE VALVES.

No.		Sizes	2	3
1	Single Socket Throttle Valve		8/6	10/6
1A	Double Socket „ „		8/6	10/6
2	Single Socket Throttle Valve with Removable Top ...		9/-	11/-
2A	Double Socket „ „ „ ...		9/-	11/-
3	H Piece with 2 Valves		27/6	32/-
3A	„ „ „ „ all Socket		27/6	32/-
4	Tee Piece with 2 Throttle Valves, two socket			

The changing landscape of work: the 1970's had seen the derelict Vulcan works site adapted as a coach business and the far end taken over by Turnbull's scrapyard which retained the Vulcan name before being swept away by the A66 carriageway. Offices were built on the entire site in the 1990's then many of these were later converted into apartments.

Thomas Allan and Sons came from their Glasgow base in 1872 setting up the Bon Lea Foundry to make gas, water and drain pipes. Many of the workers moved down from Scotland with them. By 1892 The Bon Lea employed 200 people. Allan's built houses for their workers, Glasgow Street the main street came to be known as " Scotch Row." Here residents were celebrated for their toughness and no nonsense attitude to life. However the houses were tied to the job: no work could mean no home.

The Bon Lea c1910, a range of items is being cast. Foundries would have change little by 1947 when Bill Pickering finished his apprenticeship.

The derelict Bon Lea main offices and works in 2016, this is the only part of Industrial Thornaby that remains. Above, office staff in 1950 under the same sign.

Bill Pickering's experience would be common to most of the Thornaby foundries. He began as an apprentice moulder at 14 at Crosthwaites where his father worked. When he started at Kinnells in 1947 Bill was an experienced moulder:

Thornaby was big in foundries, most of the people worked in the foundries and it was mainly family, fathers worked in the foundry and the sons followed them in. Moulding was a very skilled job and if you weren't any good they'd finish you.

The pipes were always a two man job, it was a long box and you needed two men, one at either end to lift. You had a wood pattern, you put the wood pattern on the board, then you put the moulding box over it. You had a cast iron box top and a bottom. You'd put your bottom half on and ram it up with sand and windy rammers, (a pneumatic rammer) then turn it over. We worked to very fine tolerances, you hadn't much margin for error. The furnace foreman would come round in the morning and ask how much iron you wanted, you might have a job of just over a ton, so he had to count up how much to put on the furnace, he went right round the foundry so he knew how much everybody wanted iron wise. The vat boiler was over a ton, a ton of metal, you had a crane ladle with a wheel. It

was non stop work and we worked fast, you had to, you had to get a turn on the furnace programme. It was all piece work. When you got your job the rate fixer would come down and ask you what you wanted for it. He'd have his idea of a price and you'd have to more or less fight for your price knowing that you'd have to make a day's pay out of it . You had to gauge how long the job would take but you tried to keep a little bit in hand because nothing ever went smoothly. You could pull a pattern out and you'd get what we called a bad draw and you'd have to do a lot of patching up. Everything had to go right for you to make that job pay. You all mucked in. If anyone was in trouble you'd leave your own job and go and help somebody out who was in bother. We got a great satisfaction, when you walked out and you looked in the dressing shop you could see what you'd made the day before, there was a pride that you took in your job: "I made that." BILL PICKERING

We had to live at 22 Read Street in my grandmas' house because my father had to leave the house in Glasgow street when he finished with the Bon Lea. Iron got into Dad's eye at work and he was blinded in one eye. So he never got another job, he couldn't go to the other foundries like Kinnell's because he wasn't able to do the work, he didn't even get a labouring job. There was eight of us in a three bedroom house. The Bon Lea had a social club for the workers with billiard rooms. They also had their own football team, they used to come out of the club and walk down the back street to the field at the back called Bon Lea field, they used to play on there. Some used to be in the union, they put a little table at the gable end of Glasgow Street and when the men came out they used to put coppers on the table for the dues and enter it in a book, they weren't allowed to do it in the works. You could see all the flames, not far away. As a child looking down through the gate you'd see black smoke and a red glow, you'd see men with leather aprons, it was frightening down there.
PAT STOKES (Gillgallon)

Above, the Bon Lea yard in about 1910 with stocks of pipes ready for despatch. Through the mist a rare view of Whitwell's Ironworks

My grandmother Catherine Booth, born 1905 in Ireland with her neighbour Miss Veronica McKearney on the right waiting for the Gazettes on Reed Street in 1973. Catherine lived at 22 Glasgow Street in the row of Bon Lea Foundry company houses behind her and where I was born in 1947. My grandfather Robert Booth was a foundryman. When Bob left the declining Bon Lea in the 1960's to work at Haverton Hill shipyard he couldn't believe the extra money he was earning. Catherine died in 1982, Bob died in 1989 aged 84, his death certificate records the cause as "Industrial Disease of Pneumoconiosis." DOUGIE FAIRBAIRN

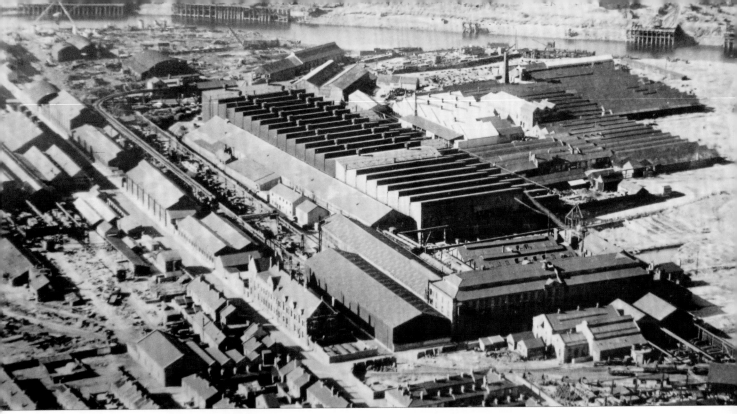

Some six foundries could be found at Teesdale: Head Wrightson ran five including a vast steel foundry and Crosthwaites Foundry which produced light iron items such as kitchen stoves, boilers, fireplaces and guttering. Like Thomas Allans they had come from Scotland, from Falkirk, a centre of iron foundry expertise in 1878. At their peak Crosthwaite's employed three hundred people.

There was a few hundred people working at Heads in the foundries, there was maintenance crews, electricians, fitters, plumbers, moulders, moulders in the core making department, people on the sand mixers, fettlers, an inspection and testing department with ultra sonic testers and visual testing as well. It was a complex process. DOUG HAUXWELL

Fettlers at Head Wrightson during the 1920's grinding a cog casting. Fettlers removed imperfections in the raw casting, smoothing down joins and seams. A fettler's work was arduous and was once performed in the open air in all weathers without masks or ear defenders.

Ronnie Brown, pattern maker using a Wadkin Router to finely trim a wood pattern made for steel castings.

Foundry team including second left back row Tommy Heslop: filling a core with sand about 1950.

Retirement presentation on the Core floor, Head Wrightson foundry about 1958. A team of women worked at the neighbouring shop making cores and can be seen in the background. Far right corner, white shirt, Neil Hampton, then in glasses Geordie Cox, core maker. Others include moulders Bob Metcalfe, Jimmy Simpson, Ted Smith and Johnny Kemp.

Workmen in the Bridge Yard about 1900.

The Teesdale industrial complex photographed in 1955. Trafalgar Street was the spine of Head Wrightson connecting a range of workshops. By this time HW was the only occupant of the site, Whitwell's Iron foundry and the two main shipyards once based at the bottom of Trafalgar Street, Richardson Duck and Craig Taylor are now grassed over.

Head Wrightson

Head Wrightson was Thornaby's main employer. A world renowned engineering company established in 1867 on the Carrs, the Teesside based sites eventually employed 4000 people at Teesdale, Stockton and Middlesbrough with over 1200 at Teesdale, for 100 years it thrived. Many of the bridges, piers and viaducts they built across the world are still in use today. Early on Head Wrightson established themselves as a global company building bridges, blast furnaces and mining installations in Africa, India, America and Europe, nothing seemed beyond the skills and ingenuity of the Teesdale site. Most of all Head Wrightson was celebrated for it's workplace camaraderie.

It was a family firm, everybody got on like a family, your father worked there, your brother, your cousins, everybody worked there. You went out together for a drink you even played football together, cricket together, table tennis for the club, they had a nice social club, with dances and everybody met together and then they went to work together.
DON LACKENBY

Two of four wrought iron bowstring girders being installed at Barnes Bridge by a modestly crewed gang in 1895. The bridge remains a key route across the river Thames and an impressive London landmark now with listed status.

The construction of the Empress Bridge over the river Sutlej Indus Valley Railway, India 1875. The work inspired Rudyard Kipling's " The Bridge Builders"

From it's very earliest days Head Wrightson became international, no doubt about that. In the safe at Head Wrightson there were some Manaus Harbour debentures, worth nothing now except as memorabilia but they had been accepted in the days of Sir Thomas Wrightson as part payment for building the harbour at Manaus which is a thousand miles up the Amazon. JOHN ECCLES

Head Wrightson installed many pit heads and pit equipment across Britain including the Ashley Green pit head 1898, the last pit in Lancashire, now restored and preserved as a listed building.

Many of Britain's best seaside piers were constructed by Head Wrightson and most are still being enjoyed. The company also installed dock gates and harbour equipment. A crew install a pier at Dover at the turn of the century.

They say that if you had an apprenticeship from Head Wrightson you could go anywhere. If you served your time at Head Wrightson's you could go to any firm in the country or any firm in the world and you'd get a start because you were skilled. Nothing can beat doing your time and learning from people with skills.

Apprentices 1965. Training at Head Wrightson was rigorous but produced highly skilled workers,

It was all done in the bridge Yard, which was a complex set up really. Starting from template making where we first started off as apprentices in the Bridge Yard, from the template shop the templates came to the young lads to mark off the beams, the joists. We used to have wooden templates, put them on the beams pop holes in them for the drillers to drill out and then that was shipped to different parts of Head Wrightson's to be built. It was rather complex but it worked like a dream. Everything was connected. Every job you did was a pride job. Everything you did was absolutely tip top, it had to be. HARRY FOSTER

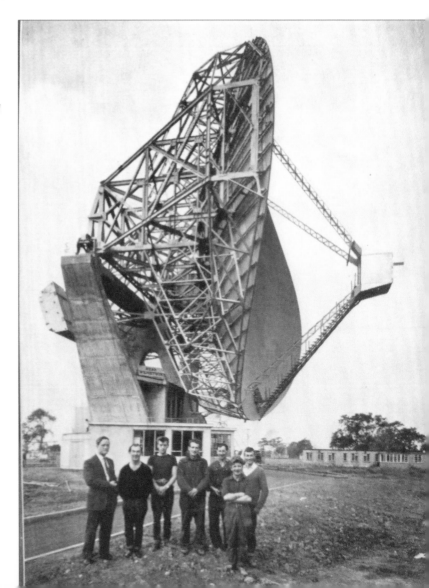

An example of Head Wrightson's diverse ability to handle any kind of commission. An Installation team with the Mark Two radio telescope at Jodrell Bank, Cheshire, in 1964, a feat of engineering accuracy built under difficult conditions. It is now a grade 1 listed building. D.A.Cartwright, site engineer with Paddy Gehan, Brian Blake, Bill Kelly, John Lacy, Bunny Morris and Colin Williams.

The President of India Dr Prasad thanks
Peter Wrightson for the company's work.
The firm built the country's first steel plants
installing four blast furnaces at the Durgapur
works, enabling India to make it's own steel.
The plant later became Tata Steel which
took over British Steel at Redcar.

Many of the steel plants installed in the
UK were built by the firm. Above, a steel
plant under construction 1950's

Many women workers could still be found in the foundries and as drillers and welders after the war,
often earning half a man's wage. Pat Allison puts the last rivet in the 1948 bascule bridge, the first in
the world to be made of aluminium, built for Hendon Dock at Sunderland, assisted by Jacky Burton.

Outside the Collingwood Hotel on Trafalgar Street about 1951.

There was a good social life you knew that many people. Some of The young ones decided after the war they'd start up a youth club so they organised a trip to Whitley Bay. Major Miles the MD got to know and he said we'll pay for the buses and we'll pay for the lunch and we all had a trip out to Whitley Bay. ENID THIRLWELL

Retired workers talk about the strong sense of community at Head Wrightson. Die Shop workers on lunch break including George Lee, Ben Hook and Ken Lamb, 1950's

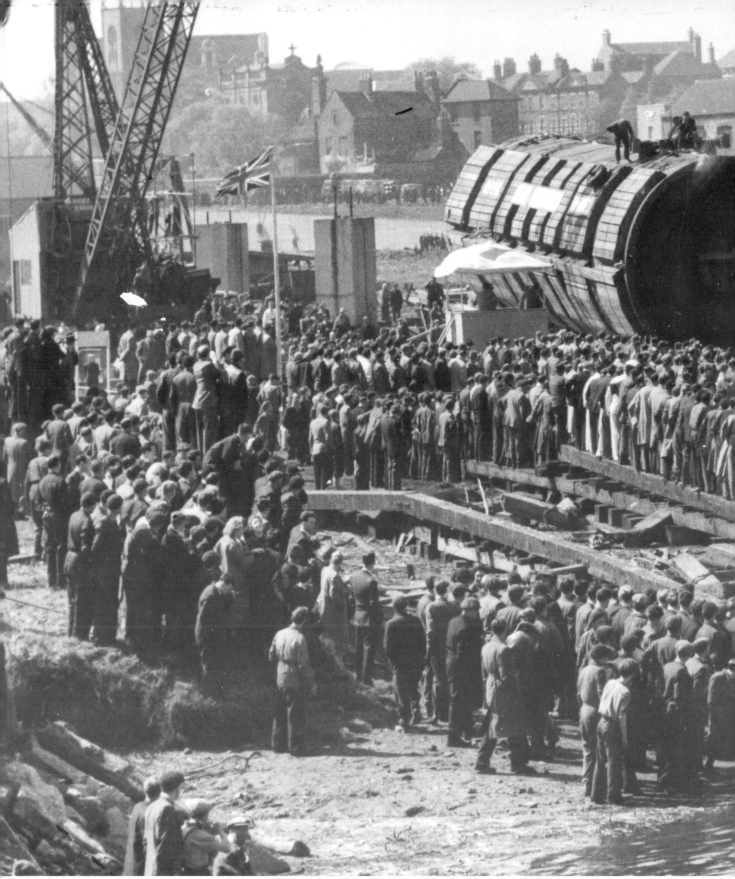

The first Bradwell nuclear heat exchanger ready to be launched on it's journey by river and sea to Essex, 1958.

The company flourished after the war and made an enormous contribution to the modernisation of key industries such as coal, steel and rail. Petrochemical and Chemical industries also commissioned major structures. Then during the late 1950's senior management saw potential in the emerging nuclear industries. The contracts were lucrative and labour intensive and they kept the Teesdale work force busy for ten years. Head Wrightson became part of a consortium that built several nuclear power plants such as Bradwell in Essex. All was backed up by the remarkably skilled engineers, metallurgists and research and development departments at Teesdale that made Head Wrightson world class.

As apprentices we were working five days a week, Saturday mornings and Sundays and two nights over and then going to night school as well. There was a lot of work around in the early 50's, you had to learn quickly because you were doing a man's job when you were a boy. There was a tremendous range of equipment that we could produce, we could turn 27 foot diameter, nearly 100 foot long, there was a lot of skilful work, a lot of skilful people in Head Wrightson. When you're launching 800 ton out in the river Tees and you're towing it out to Africa as dock gate or something of that nature, it takes skill, these were tremendous achievements, not seen any more.

BARRY PREECE

Thornaby Station

Thornaby station was arguably the best example of Victorian architecture in the town but it also became a symbol of it's industrial decline. By 1981 when the station was demolished much of Victorian Thornaby was disappearing with the virtual abandonment of the Town Hall, 19th century foundries, schools and pubs. This magnificent piece of architecture had been crucial to the development of the town linking Thornaby to the network of routes that crossed the country, you could reach most areas of Britain by train when the 1882 station opened and most goods were transported by rail. The station replaced a smaller stop near Darlington Street where the first train had arrived in 1830, across an elegant suspension bridge. The station was first called South Stockton until the town was created by Royal Charter and became a municipal Borough in 1892 and re- named Thornaby. A few years earlier. The Pease family had been keen to extend the Stockton railway, famously launched when George Stephenson drove an engine to Stockton coal staithes on the opposite bank of the river in 1825. The aim was to reach the Docks at Middlesbrough busy servicing ironstone mining, and later iron and steel production on a large scale, fortunately Thornaby was on the route and it was decided to create a halt at the emerging industrial town of South Stockton Built by the North Eastern Railway company and located around one of the busiest sections of the route, NER was enjoying success and paid a successful dividend of over 8% at the time, they had ambitions for Thornaby and the result was a lavish construction, costing £11,400- a vast sum at the time but a reflection of this time of plenty on the railway. Thornaby station also showed how labour intensive railways were, the essential skilled workers had to be housed and offices were created for telegraph operators, ticket collectors, booking and telegraph clerks, and the porters. The station had four waiting rooms serving a range of customers, apart from generous storage rooms, the original plans included a left luggage office and a parcels office.

Top, a train arrives from Darlington, 1977. The ornate iron spandrels of the roof support which helped to making the station platforms so light were individually designed.

The above photograph shows the scale of the building's construction. The double doors on the left opened up into the forecourt and goods were taken through to waiting trucks or carts. Until the 1950's rail was the most common form of goods transport, items regularly included livestock. Opposite the platform on the Town Hall side was a separate platform called Horse Dock, here horses for Stockton Races and travelling circus animals could be offloaded. Animals could be transported anywhere on the network, in 1925 for example it cost 23 shillings and four pence to send a horse to Aberdeen.

A steam train arrives from Middlesbrough at the Darlington and Newcastle platform 1950.

Thornaby was a busy thoroughfare, a steam train with mineral cargo passes by probably on it's way to the vast iron and steel plants further down the line. The Station Master and foreman show off their beds of vividly coloured snapdragons taken around 1950. The glass in the station canopy behind them was smashed in one of the nearby air raid bomb blasts.

Easily missed and eight feet about floor level, a band of sandstone carvings ran around the whole building for some 500 feet and this is what made Thornaby unique. Each six foot section was separately hand carved and there were 104 of these different motifs altogether. The product of an apprentice stone mason's competition, the quality of the stone carving is a testament to the remarkably high standard of Victorian craftsmanship.

Left, Thornaby station never reached it's centenary. Major upgrading was necessary by a cash strapped British Rail being prepared for privatisation. It was decided to demolish the entire building in 1981 despite protests from preservation groups. Three original stone motifs preserved at Preston Hall Museum are all that survives of Thornaby station.

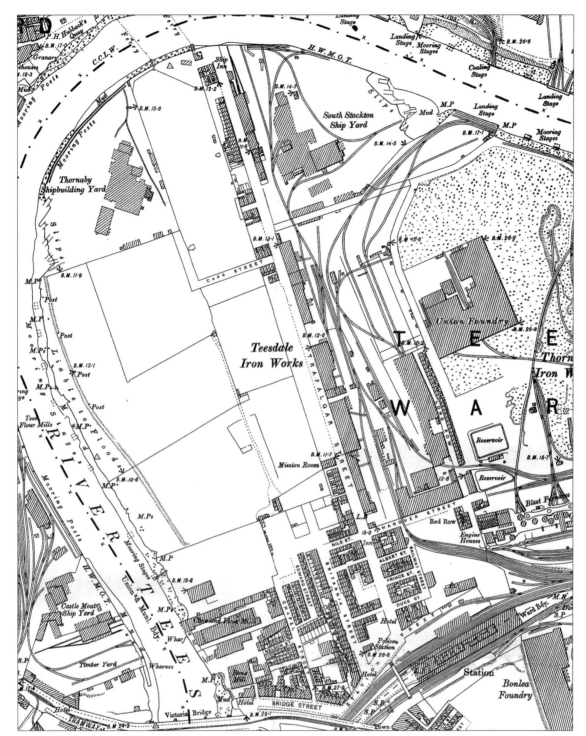

Below the Railway

Very little existed on the bend in the river once called The Carrs and later Teesdale apart from horse racing until industry began to develop in the mid 19th Century. Richardson Duck established a shipyard in 1854, The Teesdale Iron Works began in 1840 on an acre of land and later became Head Wrightson in 1864. Good links by river and rail helped Teesdale become Thornaby's industrial hub. A close knit community mainly of Irish immigrants developed separated from the rest of the emerging town by the railway and where work was literally on the doorstep.

Some workers restored themselves with non alcoholic drinks after the sweat of the foundry or the Bridgeyard at Heads. The Sheldon shop and home on Trafalgar Street is typical of the mid 19th Century housing of Teesdale. Mary Ann Sheldon with George Henry Sheldon who holds their grandson William about 1905.

Above, Britannia Street,1936. Centre, Sheila Bonner and Connie Tunney who holds Cath Harrison. Many in this group including Cath, left in photo on left in about 1948 would start their working lives at Head Wrightson. Cath helped to build rolling stock for British Rail after the war.

When my mam died of pneumonia just after the war, and this is what it was like below the railway, we all had to get our clothes dyed black for her funeral. Then the people over the road, there was six of them like us, their father had been out of work and he'd died and they borrowed all our clothes to wear for their father's funeral. A lot of people looked down their noses if you lived below the railway, and never visited. I always said " You don't know what you've missed " They were marvellous people down there, everyone was so neighbourly.
CATH HARRISON

Work and homes. A terrace at the North End of Trafalgar Street faces industrial workshops. At the wooden sign below the lamp is the Bradford Vaults pub.

When the hammer went in the Blacksmith's Shop – it shook our house because we were so close to Head Wrightson's. When we were kids we used to go down to the wharf to slide down the slag tips. There was no signs saying you can't go here. As long as the steam engine wasn't coming across the Trafalgar Street railway lines. But it was just part of our livelihood really. That's how we grew up with Head Wrightson's CATH HARRISON

A communal life. A bus trip assembles outside The Commercial in 1931 the largest of seven pubs below the railway.

A heavy load from Head Wrightson negotiates Bridge Street in 1958. Thornaby Town Hall top right. Number 35 is second house from left.

Bridge Street were all railway houses, the residents were all railway workers, I was born in 35 Bridge Street, two up two down, outside toilets, a backyard, my nana made a garden in the back yard she had me carrying soil from Mrs Sudders out the back. My grandfather George worked on the railway, by the time he retired in 1965 he had done 52 years service including his forces time and secondment to Buenos Aires, Argentina. When my granddad retired it was my job to get his pension and I used to go down the station to collect it from Thornaby Station ticket office. "Can I have granddad's pension please." 52 years, it was about five or six shillings a week. He never even got a watch. He died when he was 73 so he had 8 years retirement, he died the year we came up to the Dales Estate, 1964 he never set foot in the new bungalow where my Nana was re housed to but Nana brought his coffin up there from the hospital so he was buried from the new house. Everybody was railway mad, down the station train spotting, all the kids who were my friends their dads were all drivers.
You could leave your doors open, it was a great place to grow up. I was a best friend with Dougie Leeman who lived in Garden Place, he was a cousin of Richard Griffiths who was born there, his mother was a Griffiths and Richard was born in number one Garden Place. His sisters were older and they were all deaf, he was the only one who could speak. I remember him as a kid coming down the steps to see his auntie Nellie.
ERIC WHITFIELD

Right, Eva and Georgina Walker, 1974, sisters who ran first the Burton Arms and then the Collingwood Hotel on Trafalgar Street. One of the most popular meeting places and the last of seven pubs to survive below the railway, The Collingwood was demolished in 1988 in spite of a campaign to save it

We lived in Edward Street everybody knew each other, you never locked your door and all the neighbours sat out on the steps, the kids played out and the parents sat in their chairs. Dad worked at the flour mill he would come out all white, covered in flour and pick me up, especially his face because they had no shower or anything there and we only had a back yard with a tin bath so it was a nightmare. Dad later got TB somehow.

My mam had 11 children only 6 of us lived, I remember a brother then a sister after me then a baby after that and I remember walking in there to the parlour where they slept and meeting one of the women up the street who delivered, you often didn't go for a midwife, and her coming out with something under her arm, it was a stillborn. If anyone was getting buried it was shoved in their coffin.

We were playing out one day with my friends the Wincups, Margaret Wincup had a little sister and she stepped out from the curb and a flour mill lorry was coming out and went over her. She was absolutely gorgeous, they never touched her face and we were all taken in to see her in her coffin. A little white coffin, she lived in Garden Place and when we went in there was this baby dressed in silk . They used to say "She's too beautiful to live she had to be a little angel." we kids were scared stiff, this baby has died, this must have been when I was 7 or younger. ETHEL TYREMAN

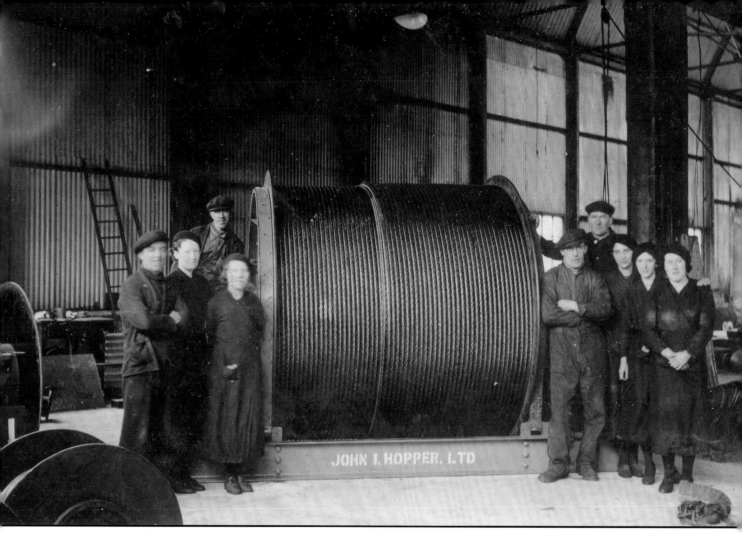

Hoppers

John I. Hopper at the Cleveland Ropery on Brewery Bank was the last factory to make steel ropes on Teesside. A family business established in 1894 Hoppers made heavy duty steel ropes, clients included mines, the Admiralty, engineering, earth moving and shipping industries. Many of the products were exported world wide. The firm appears to have moved from Thornaby in the late 60's. A last major contract involved supplying wire slings used for installing the reactor at Dungeness Nuclear Power Station which had a capacity of 400 tons.

A group at Hopper's September 1936. Front right is William Peacock of Westbury Street, next to him is May Danks and her sister Lilly who was to marry William six months later. William's father had also worked at Hopper's since before the first World War.

Lilly Peacock completed her working life in brighter if less characterful surroundings as manager of a dry cleaners in George Street, 1965.

Hoppers Ropeworks, bottom right in this aerial photograph which includes most of Thornaby's industry about 1960.

1. Head Wrightson.   2. Crosthwaites Foundry   7. N.E.Brewery site.   8. Richardson Duck site.
3. Bon Lea Foundry.   4. Clevo Flour Mill   9. Craig Taylor site.   10. Thornaby Station
5. Whitwell Iron site.   6.Hoppers Ropeworks   11.Town Hall.   12. Pumphreys

I ended up working in Hoppers Ropery in 1954 making steel rope. In a morning when you went in it was all quiet until the machines struck up, these big weaving machines turned the steel string thicker and thicker that eventually ended up with all the various thicknesses of steel rope. The noise was phenomenal, everyone shouted and there were no ear defenders. I was splicing the ropes, we were in a big steel shed but there was no heating except scattered in a couple of different areas some potbellied stoves after three foot it was absolutely freezing cold. I got the job but the foreman didn't like me. This day he came round when I was warming my hands round the fire and he said "Get back to work you!" I was a bit cheeky in those days and said " Stick your job!" He said I'm clocking you off and I walked off the job. So now I'm really in the mud. When I got home my father said the same thing " I'm not keeping you if you're not going to work." I was in the ATC as a boy and there wasn't an airplane I couldn't identify, I was always interested in aircraft. Most of my leisure time I'd be on the airfield sitting on the barricade watching the vampires. I said to my dad "I'm going to join the RAF." He said okay. I went and took the Queens shilling down at the recruitment office and signed on. Dad said "You won't be able to walk away from that !" I didn't realise at the time what he meant.
HENRY GODWIN

Whitwell's Iron Works

There was often a price to pay for industrial production: the photograph on the left of Whitwell's taken after it closed suggests the impact of pollution on residential Thornaby; works accidents were common everywhere, eight people were killed at Whitwells over the years and many more injured. Run by several generations of the related Quaker families of Pease and Whitwell, Thornaby Iron Works dominated the landscape with it's three, eighty foot blast furnaces. Established in 1859 to make pig iron it spread across 68 acres, and at it's peak employed 700 men producing 100,000 tons of iron annually. There was also six rolling mills and extensive coke ovens. Ore was unloaded and iron ingots exported by ship at the nearby private wharf on the Tees, ore could also be brought to the site via a siding with four miles of track connected to the main line and to the wharf. The works had a poor health and safety record, some of the eight people killed over the years succumbed to horrific deaths including Thomas Whitwell, the director and inventor who was burned to death in August 1878.

Above, the blast furnaces 1905. Gelignite was used in 1935 to demolish the furnaces. Once they produced 1000 tons of hematite iron a week but Post War conditions such as the glut of pig iron and the price of coal left the company bankrupt by 1922. The site was finally sold for £9000 in 1942 to Cork Insulation and Asbestos after a substantial slag tip had been cleared .

Whitwell's taken from the Flour Mill about 1933. Trafalgar Street runs across the foreground

Boiler explosion 1870's

Director William Whitwell was one of the first Mayors of the new Borough in 1896

Picture Houses

Cinema going in Thornaby was an important part of community life. Working people had limited leisure time available, the cinema could also be an escape from everyday challenges. The bill changed twice each week and most patrons viewed both films, in fact they could see four films weekly since each feature had a supporting B film. A night out at the Pictures could be good value in 1951 at four pence a ticket for a three hour visit. When the Queens Cinema was demolished in 1976 it's daybooks were rescued by Teesside Archives, they reveal a unique record of a half century of cinema going in Thornaby.

The Queens on Mandale Road was converted from the Market Hall to the Edisonia Cinema in 1913 and became the Queens about 1924. Above refurbishment, 1951 during the post war cinema boom, this included new windows, offices and a canopy for waiting queues to shelter under. The Queens had stalls and a circle with 700 seat capacity.

I used to go in the Queens Picture house on my own and I'd go in for the first house, there was two showings of the same film and I'd stay to watch them both. I used to be down the front and I'd always fall asleep. My sister Gladys used to come looking for me. There was a doorman with a proper uniform on: "He's down there at the front fast asleep." The Central matinees on a Saturday were packed with Hop Along Cassidy and Tom and Jerry cartoons and Batman and cowboys. We'd come out into the daylight and everyone rushed home and played cowboys and indians. NORMAN FULTON

The Queens Cinema was held in great affection by the town. Managed by the Peacock family and owned by Simeon Whitworth Nightingale who can be seen at the window on the top right. In June 1956 local residents were given a grandstand view of Queen Elizabeth as she briefly passed by the Mandale Road cinema on her way to Thornaby Race Course.

The Queens was never a fleapit, I heard that from people who used to call the Central the fleapit as it was old but it too was a very comfortable little cinema with nice jolly staff. It was a lonely job in the projection room, you're watching your projectors making sure the carbons are properly set, that they haven't worn out, that the machine runs correctly, the reels aren't too tight, no funny noises going through. You had to stand by your machine and watch it go through. You also had to watch your curtains, you drew the curtains, put the records on in the intervals, you had to draw the curtains at the right time, and fade the lights. You had to do the whole lot. FRED HICKS, projectionist.

The word got out that it was a good film, Quo Vadis or something like that with Victor mature or John Wayne. Then everybody would head to the picture house to get in the queue to go in. The picture house filled up and you'd get to the front of the queue and the cinema was full! So you'd stand there and wait for the second performance. People would stand in the rain with umbrellas talking to each other waiting for somebody to come out. The Usher would come along the queue and say " There's one seat." And when you went in everybody smoked so the whole theatre was full of smoke, it was like walking into a fog. The beam used to shine through the fog, it was like a lighthouse beacon. Looking back at the films now some of them were terrible. But the picture house were always full. HENRY GODWIN

Archibald and Archibald's architectural drawing of the Mayfair cinema. Unlike the other two cinemas it was purpose built and in a relatively lavish art deco style in 1938.

Mayfair staff, summer, 1949, from left: Manageress Hilda Evans, Mrs Ruth Clarke, Edith, Mrs Kyle, projectionist Wilf Gash, seated Marie Cotton and Mrs Dorothy Coates.

The advent of Television in the late 1950's and early 60's finished off cinema going in Thornaby. For example the takings for the Central Hall's final film, "The Hong Kong Affair" in August 1958 came to just £10 on it's final Friday night. The buildings remained active apart from the derelict Central. Both the Queens which ended film programmes in 1962 and the Mayfair, below, operated as successful bingo halls.

The Central Hall began showing films in about 1912 and at 1500 seats with a gallery as well as circle and stalls had the largest capacity in the town although the gallery appears to have been too far from the screen and rarely used. The last performance was in August 1958. It was demolished in 1977 to make way for the A66 carriageway.

S.W. Nightingale came to Thornaby from Ormskirk and gave up his job as an engineering draughtsman to make a success of running both the Queens and Central Cinemas during the 1920's until the end of their lives. After the war Mr Nightingale also ran the Mayfair Cinema. He commissioned a film of the 1928 Carnival which is now lost, on the following pages are some surviving frames. Below a fancy Dress competition in Victoria Recreation ground.

People flocked to the screenings at both cinemas for a chance to see themselves on the screen. The original negative stored in the office was stolen along with other films Mr. Nightingale had commissioned from Debenham's of York. These frames were printed from fragments discovered in the derelict office of the Queens Cinema before demolition. They give us a rare glimpse of a remarkably vibrant community.

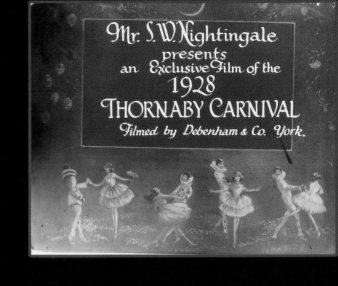

Mr. S. W. Nightingale
presents
an Exclusive Film of the
1928
THORNABY CARNIVAL
Filmed by Debenham & Co. York.

Held to raise funds for Stockton and Thornaby Hospital this annual event over several days brought the whole town out onto the streets. A King and Queen arrived by boat at the Trafalgar Street pier and were met by the Mayor who gave them a key to the town. The couple led a spectacular procession through the town to the Victoria Recreation Ground where judging of the many decorated competitions took place.

Left Oxford Road, below, Fancy Dress: a costume made from Woodbine cigarette packets.

The King and Queen in Ruritanian costume lead the procession along Francis Street in open landau at the corner of Queen Street. A succession of revellers follow them including Fancy Costumes, decorated Motors, Horse Vehicles, Cycling Clubs, Piper's Band and Tableaux.
The barefoot child in the foreground, right, is a reminder of the depravation some families were experiencing in 1928 Thornaby, already in depression after the failure of key industries.

Best Fancy Dress for Men :
Joe Mead as a pygmy.

New Street looking towards the station.

York Street, the costumed figure on the far right was recently identified as William Mead who came to work in Thornaby from Bow and remained in the town. The curved window behind on the left is the old Carnegie public Library and survives today, this site now hosts the Eastern Sunrise Bakery

Public Health

Poverty and overcrowding in slums were breeding grounds for fevers and the 1900 photograph of Spring Street families becomes an interesting document when linked to Dr Watson's map of the scarlet fever epidemic of 1892-3 because Victor Street became Spring Street and this was the fever hotspot. The photograph portrays the typically large families of the period who lived in overcrowded bedrooms, several of the children are shoeless suggesting high levels of depravation. Later the 1902-3 diphtheria outbreak claimed the lives of 16 young people in the town.

The small isolation hospital built by the Council to deal with the 1898 small pox outbreak. Dr Watson, argued for more units to cope with regular fever outbreaks but this appears to have been the last built. The work could be hazardous for nurses like Louisa Leeson, right, who was also often treated as a pariah in the town because of her contact with the infected patients.

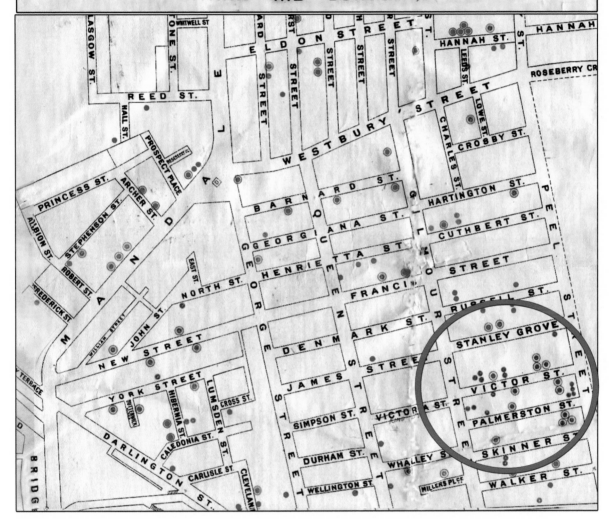

BOROUGH OF THORNABY ON TEES
INFECTIOUS DISEASES
PLAN.
SHEWING LOCALITIES OF INFECTIOUS DISEASES WITHIN THE BOROUGH,

Thornaby was once a myriad of health hazards: diphtheria, scarlet fever, tuberculosis were common. The council appointed a Medical Officer of Health in 1893 to advise. Dr Thomas Watson and his quarterly reports give a remarkable insight into the town at a time when outbreaks of infectious diseases were rife. Sadly there was modest resources at his disposal. Folk remedies and charitable institutions made up a lot of the provision for the low income population, until the Compulsory Health Insurance 1911 Act when low paid workers finally had access to doctors and hospitals. Employers and employees also paid subscriptions to local doctors. However it wasn't until 1948 with the introduction of the National Health Service that the people of Thornaby finally received proper health care.

I met our Ray on the stairs at ten o clock he was going to bed early with a mug of hot milk in his hand, he wasn't well. Then at about 11.30 his wife screamed down, he was very ill, he was delirious. Me and me mam went to get the doctor, we knocked and knocked at this door and couldn't get any answer, even though there was a dim light on. We sat on the wall by the railings outside Rounds the Chemist in despair, wondering what the hell we could do, Mam was in tears. It was well past midnight. Then a Bobby on his beat asked what we were doing out at that time of night. The bobby took us back to the doctor's house and banged really hard on the door. This time someone opened a window upstairs. "I'm afraid the doctor is not available." " Then I'll have to come in and get him, he is needed urgently." The doctor had a syringe and injected Ray with something, but that was it, he was too late, Ray just gasped and died, he was 21 years old, just married and with a child on the way. HOWARD FULTON

Pollution from the many industrial chimneys combined with the smoke from thousands of coal burning fires in Thornaby was a constant but unacknowledged health threat. The 1903 view towards Stockton from Thornaby Town Hall was most likely taken to expose the emissions from the chimney of Tees Bone Mill. The manure manufacturer was constantly being cautioned by the Council to control the appalling fumes and smells that permeated the town.

Raymond Fulton just before he died of Walking Pneumonia in 1928 with his parents Clara and Harry.

Labour MP Arthur Greenwood an
ex-Health Minister, right, opened
the Welfare Centre in January
1932, he accepts the key from
contractor LW Evans. To the MP's
left Mayor Brennan and Nurse
Mary Ramsay. The large crowd
includes many of the supporting
volunteers and indicates the extent
of local public concern for the
health of young people in the
town.

Right, Christmas party 1939.

In 1932 a Maternity and Child Welfare Centre in Francis Street was opened by the
council and it became a life saver. Dr. Watson's 1913 chart revealed an infantile
mortality rate of one in seven and the Welfare was one of the responses to these
shocking statistics. The centre included Tuberculosis and School clinics under the
auspices of the County Council. Advice was given to mothers in ante and post natal
sessions, supplies of powdered baby milk, orange juice, cod liver oil and nappies
were distributed. Most importantly each infant was weighed monthly and
monitored for signs of ill health and children were immunised for diseases such as
diphtheria, in the middle of the depression threats such as malnutrition were ever
present, the centre met the challenges with an army of female volunteers led by
Nurse Mary Ramsay.

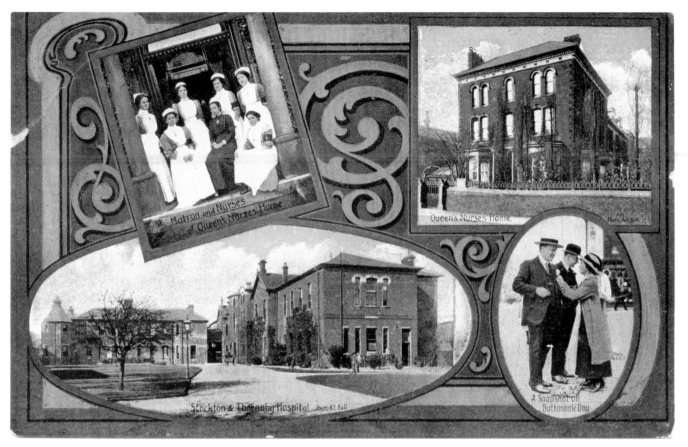

Volunteer hospitals like Stockton and Thornaby founded in 1875 made up over 30% of health provision. This was a well equipped hospital but with only 178 beds in 1920 to serve a combined population of 83,000. The public voluntary charity depended on philanthropy and contributory schemes from patients to provide the main funding. Events like the Thornaby Carnivals were organised to raise money for the hospital; local benefactors like Mrs C.W. Littleboy regularly provided substantial funds.

The female ward at Stockton and Thornaby Hospital 1913, back left, Florence Spence.

Erimus Cottages:1872-1959

Next stop Erimus Cottages. An unusual photograph taken from the top of a passing tram in about 1900. The Erimus Hotel is just visible at the vanishing point beyond the top right of the tram, the shape of the racecourse stands can be made out on the far right.

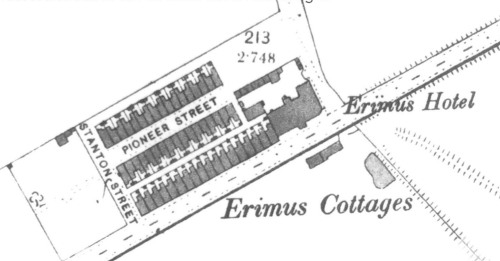

Erimus Cottages an isolated close knit community of three terraces on the Middlesbrough Road, or "Wilderness" between Middlesbrough and Thornaby was built to house the workers of the short lived Erimus Iron Company of 1872 and became almost a community in microcosm. The racecourse opposite provided extra work for residents. Because of the flood plane it never developed beyond the three streets yet it thrived until 1959 without facilities like mains electricity. A visit by the Medical Officer of Health led to the 56 homes being condemned.

Ronnie Thompson and Jim Pemberton on Middlesbrough Road, in the background the Erimus Hotel about 1955 just before it was demolished. The Hotel was unusually grand in relation to the small community of the Erimus, it was built mainly to serve racecourse clients.

There was a little shop, there was a pub, a little chapel. It was self-sustaining you might say and it was surrounded by allotments. There was also a wood factory making firelighters run by Harry and Joe Winn. It It was a good little business, they had two horses and a cart. I used to work there part-

time and help them. There was a great big diesel engine to cut the wood, it was a great beast and I think he had a couple of fingers off getting a bit too close. KEN CRAGGS

WATER KNEE-DEEP IN "WILDERNESS" HOMES

Hard days for the womenfolk

OVER in the "wilderness," as Tees-side calls the stretch of land between Thornaby and Middlesbrough, the people who live in the well-known row of houses at the Erimus have already had a grim foretaste of what the winter may have in store for them.

Flooding, caused by high tides, has for long been a problem to them. This year they hoped that the work done by Thornaby Town Council in repairing the banks of the Old River (which flows into the Tees) would solve their difficulties.

But it was not to be. Since last week-end they have been living in anxiety of the water rising through the drains. Taken unawares by the first overflow last Saturday, they have since then kept constant watch at high-water periods.

Our pictures were taken on Wednesday, the worst day so far. After the early morning tide water was knee-deep in some of the rooms. At the Erimus Hotel it was five feet deep in the beer cellar.

And after each flood comes the cleaning-up. They're hard days for the men and women of the Erimus.

ELEVEN MONTHS OLD Christine Foxall being rescued after being marooned with her mother in an upstairs bedroom during the height of the flood. The urgency was the baby's breakfast

NINETY-YEAR-OLD Mr. Sedgewick and 85-year-old Mrs. Stamp seen in the lobby of one of the affected houses after they had won their battle with the flood water.

THE scene in the grocer's shop (above) at the end of the terrace which was badly affected as the floating biscuit tins, etc., show. The local Food Officer was needed to check the stock for damage. LEFT: Furniture propped-up on chairs in one of the dwelling rooms.

Above, serious flooding reported in the North Eastern Weekly News October 28, 1949.

It was a tremendously close knit community, a lot of the people who lived there were actually related to each other. So you could go into someone's house and she was your auntie. But even the people who weren't got on. Everybody had an allotment at the back of the houses and everybody kept hens. If you went from the Erimus towards Middlesbrough, two fields away from the houses was the old river. It wasn't a very big river but it was tidal and it went in to the River Tees about a mile away from the Erimus And if you got a high Spring tide coming from the tidal Tees pushing water up the old river that coincided with a lot of rain further up the old river then a lot of water was coming down, a lot of water was coming up, it just flooded over into the fields and occasionally flooded the houses. ALAN CLARK

If you look at old photographs of people from the 1940's there was no fat people about they were very slim because they did so much work. My grandfather was probably about 8 stone wringing wet he worked hard and had 2 allotment plots so he'd be digging hard when he wasn't at work, they were always doing something.
ALAN CLARK

Alan Clark minding racegoers bikes on race day, they were kept in his grandmother's yard. Homes that took them in chalked their back doors.

The people who were at the Erimus thought they were at the epicenter of the world, they thought the people in Thornaby were in the wilderness! The house we were born in at 3 Pioneer Street was exactly the same as the one my grandparents lived in across the road. You walked in through the front door straight in to the front room. There was one room with a range at the far side where they did all the cooking and they had a harmonium and to the left of that there was a door leading up stairs to two bedrooms. Behind the living room there was a scullery and that had a copper with a fire underneath that boiled water up if you wanted a bath. There was no electricity, just gas light and the mantles were delicate things. The colour I remember was dirty, it was an industrial environment and everything was painted brown or cream. The space was tight so multi purpose in as much as it was a bedroom as well. I remember the fadgies in a bowl rising in front of the fire. When it came to race day it was as though the world had come to the Erimus because there was so many people. My grandmother used to feed as many as came through the door, in that festive period. We delighted in asking people for a percentage of their winnings, it went along the line of " Any lucky ha'pennies mister." So we used to beg in front of the Erimus Hotel which was a vast place, in relation to the houses around it was palatial with a high ceiling. The Erimus was a place of huge contrasts and people worked round the clock to keep their head above water. I remember the sheer capacity of my grandmother to be tolerant, the community was tolerant, accepting of people, there was understanding and compassion, maybe because we belonged to a large family.
PETER CLARK

The Great War memorial plaque erected in 1920. One can imagine the impact of so many deaths on such a small community, the last two soldiers could be brothers. The plaque was in storage for years after the Erimus was demolished in 1959. Councillor Ken Craggs later led a successful campaign to build an Erimus memorial in Thornaby cemetery with the plaque as a centrepiece.

It was a mile to school but you never thought anything of it, you walked to school and walked back. If you were lucky you had a halfpenny or a penny to get on the tram. When there was snow and that sort of thing you still went to school you still had to go whatever weather it was. I even saw children without shoes walking to school in their bare feet. KEN CRAGGS

Right, the Pemberton family outside 8 Pioneer Street 1957, back, Glynis Pemberton, Joyce Permberton, Lizzie Pemberton, Violet Olsen (Pemberton) Fay Pemberton, front, Barbara Bunce, Stephen Bunce, Lesley Wickens.

A group pose for a photograph outside the Chapel during the 1937 Coronation celebrations.

I was born in the Erimus in 1949 I remember putting my hand in my shoes to make sure no blacklocks were hiding. When the flood came up my grannie moved us all up to the top bedrooms and when we looked out of the window there was blacklocks coming out of the drains, they were all floating away. The community was very close knit, everybody knew everybody, there was only a few streets . All my relatives lived there and as every one of them got married one by one they moved into my Grannie Lizzie Pemberton's front parlour until they got a house. There was eight of them and she'd lost two children in childbirth. We used to go over to the racecourse and ask for lucky ha pennies, there was me Avril Baron and Ronnie Burns, "Any lucky ha pennies sir ?" A fella gave us half a crown each, he must have won. We thought our birthdays had come.

Gypsies lived at the end of Pioneer Street where there was a bit of spare land.

We used to play with all the kids, they taught us how to make paper flowers out of toilet roll. I still remember today how to make those flowers. There was a few tents and caravans, they were there in the mid 1950's, we all used to play together, there was no prejudice. My grannie was the last one to move out of Erimus Terrace, she didn't want to move, she was so used to street houses. They offered her a place in Littleboy Drive where many of the other Erimus people were re- housed but she couldn't get used to it so she moved to York Street - a terrace back down the old end. LINDA WILSON (PEMBERTON)

The First World War

By 1917 women produced 80% of the munitions being used by the British Army and by the end of the war nearly a million women were working, like this group photographed at Head Wrightson works in Teesdale. At this time women did not have the vote but their essential role in wartime led to all women over 30 gaining the vote in 1919, but it wasn't until 1928 that the age was reduced to parity with men at 21.

Wilfred Evelyn Littleboy

In 1892 when Thornaby became the Borough of Thornaby on Tees by virtue of Royal Charter, Charles W Littleboy was elected as councillor for the Westbury Ward. Charles was a Quaker, a religion wholly opposed to violence and conflict, and so when peace was shattered many years later with the beginning of World War 1, it is said that he tried to persuade his sons, Wilfred and Charles, not to join up, but all to no avail. Wilfred Evelyn Littleboy answered the nation's call and became a lieutenant in the 16/Royal Warwickshire regiment in which he served with distinction and saw action on a number of fronts. Tragically however, Wilfred was killed on the 9th of October 1917 along with 417 battalion comrades during the attack on Polderhoek Chateau during what is familiarly called Third Ypres. Lieutenant Littleboy was only 21 years old when he died.

Cemetery and ruined church in Gheluvelt 1917 | Mrs C.W. Littleboy

The Colonel Commanding the 16th Warwicks wrote a letter of condolence to Lieutenant Littleboy's parents which said: "I cannot speak too highly of your son's work since he joined me. He was one of the best Officer's it has been my privilege to command, and his loss is a very great one both to me personally and to my Battalion. As you have no doubt heard, it was his Platoon that won the cup for the best Platoon in the Division and he led them as well in action as he did in winning the competition. He was most popular with his men who knew they had a man fit to lead them and they are as grieved at his loss as I am. He was magnificently brave. He did splendidly and died in the finest way a man can die."

Later a story arose that some time after Armistice, an English lady - Lieutenant Littleboy's mother - knocked at the door of Father Delrue, a priest at the Church of Gheluvelt in Belgium. The lady explained that her son had been killed during fighting in the area near Polderhoek Chateau and needed help in locating where he was interred. The priest was sympathetic and the following morning, accompanied by Father Delrue, an acquaintance called Pol Maertens and his helper, Henri Verstraete, the lady travelled to Polderhoek where amazingly they found her son's body buried in what is now known as Hooge Crater Cemetery XII H 4. As a measure of her gratitude, Wilfred's mother, on behalf of the Litleboy family, donated a large sum of money for the restoration of the Gheluvelt Church which now proudly displays a memorial bronze plaque to the memory of Lieutenant Wilfrid Evelyn Littleboy. In September 1930, as a further tribute to his son, Charles Littleboy donated land in Thornaby on Tees (where he was once mayor) which became what is now Littleboy Park and where it is planned that a plaque will be erected by Thornaby Town Council to his memory.

Gheluvelt Church today

G.O.Spence

Gilbert Ormerod Spence was responsible for the Thornaby Cenotaph and also some rare paintings of the war. Born in 1879 he was from a long line of shipbuilders and worked at Richardson Duck Shipyard along with his father H.G.Spence where he became a partner. At 32 he was one of the youngest councillors elected to Thornaby Borough Council in 1911 and the first councillor to be elected Mayor in 1912. At the outbreak of war Gilbert was promoted to lieutenant- colonel of the 5th Battalion Durham Light Infantry commanding until 1918 and he was active across important battles such as the Second Battle of Ypres, the Hooge gas attack in 1915, the Battle of the Somme in 1916, Arras and Flanders in1917, before being injured at Estaires in 1918 when his command came to an end. He was twice mentioned in Despatches and awarded the Distinguished Service Order for his work at the battle of the Somme. Gilbert was tragically killed in a car crash in 1925 aged 47 at Leven Bridge. He bequeathed the paintings and his unique collection of over 3,000 weapons and military memorabilia covering the Stone Age to the World War to Stockton Council, it formed the first collection at Preston Park Museum where it can now be seen.

Gilbert painted over 100 watercolours during the war of life in and out of the line and these sharply observed scenes portraying the experiences of local men are all now preserved at Preston Park Museum. He seems not to have had any art training or instruction and the works may appear primitive or child-like at times but they give us a an intimate, unsentimental portrait of the conflict.

"Durham Light Infantrymen holding on, Estaires, morning of 11th April 1918."
Gilbert Spence was shot during the battle resisting the great German offensive, his battalion showed great courage under fire holding their position in a near impossible situation. He was invalided out for the rest of the war.

Overleaf: the Portland stone Cenotaph in Harewood Pleasure Gardens whose granite tablets bear the names of 369 Thornaby citizens who lost their lives in the First World War. The monument served again after the 1939-1945 conflict. In 1920 Gilbert set up a board to raise funds for a War Memorial by public subscription and in May a leaflet was posted to every home and business in the town together with an envelope for contributions. The target of £1000, the equivalent of £45,000 today was achieved within a month Gilbert was invited to unveil the Cenotaph at a ceremony on 28th July 1921.

Left and below:
Gas Station 28th September 1917. Ruins of Albert December 1915.
Trench foot dressing station, March 6, 1916. Burial Party July 7 1917.

Of the conditions of the landscape, pen can hardly describe: here was the scene of terrific fighting: here brave Britishers had made the great sacrifice for the freedom of mankind: yonder had once stood the peaceful village of Thiepval, it was now levelled to the ground. Here and there great trees were rooted up, while others were snapped off like matchwood. Desolation – in front, behind to right and left- such was the picture presented to the eye when looking about on top….. the clouds thinned and the moon was showing a subdued light over the desolated battlefield. Surely never in the history of mankind had the face of the earth been so wantonly destroyed as had this once peaceful and prosperous village. Thursday.. Friday…. Saturday the hours flew by and at last the order came to be ready. It was 7 o clock on Saturday night, that day of which we all had happy memories of holidays and peaceful home life, of marking for the Sabbath, but tonight we were called to our duties and each man was determined to acquit himself as a soldier should: we left the rest to God. RAYMOND S. BRAITHWAITE

Raymond S.Braithwaite chose not to describe what followed when he was shot in the spine in 1917 and invalided out of the army. He had to use crutches for the rest of his life and remained in pain. The bullet was lodged permanently in his bones and in 1943 this caused a growth which led to his death aged 47. In spite of his disability Raymond who lived in Cromwell Terrace did important voluntary work in the Second World War and set up a successful travel and shipping company, he organised some of the first battlefield tours back to France and Belgium.

THIS MEMORIAL WAS ERECTED
BY PUBLIC SUBSCRIPTION
GRATEFUL REMEMBRANCE OF
THE MEN OF THORNABY-ON-TEES
WHO GAVE THEMSELVES IN THE
GREAT WAR 1914 - 1918

PTE.	B. AITHWAITE.	5TH D.L.I.
SCT.	M. J. AITHWAITE.	2ND Y.4.Ls.
PTE.	A. ANDERSON.	9TH Y.L.I.
	A. ANDERSON.	4TH K.O.Y.L.I.
	F. N. ANDERSON.	3/1 ESSEX YEO
SCT.	E. ANDREWS.	6TH YKS.
PTE.	W. ANDREWS.	A. & S. H¹.
	J. S. ATKIN.	D.L.I.
	F. J. ATKINSON.	12TH N. FUS.
	F. ATKINSON.	K. O. Y. L. I.
	J. W. AUDAS.	5TH D.L.I.
STR.	A. AYRE.	R.N.R.
PTE.	A. V. BAILEY.	D.L.I.
	J. BARTON.	1ST WORC. REC.
STR.	T. BELL.	R. N. R.
PTE.	W. BINGHAM.	LAN. FUS.
	J. H. BLACK.	6TH D.L.I.
SCT.	R. R. BLAKE.	D.L.I.
PTE.	W. BLOWMAN.	5TH D.L.I.
RFN.	J. W. BOOTH.	10TH R. B.
L/C.	R. BOOTH.	5TH D.L.I.
PTE.	A. BOSTON.	20TH D.L.I.
	J. BOYD.	13TH YKS.
	W. BONNER.	1/5TH D.L.I.
	J. T. BRADLEY.	1/5TH D.L.I.
SCT.	J. BRADLEY.	5TH D.L.I.
CPL.	L. G. BRIERLY.	R.E.
PTE.	R. BROWN.	M.G.C.
	C. N. BROWN.	10TH HSSRS.
	R. BROWN.	22ND DRMS.
	N. BUCHANAN.	2ND D.L.I.
	E. CAIRNS.	AUS. FORCES.
L/C.	G. O. CAMPBELL.	7TH YKS.
PTE.	G. CAMPION.	6TH D.L.I.
	S. CARLISLE.	M.G.C.
	F. CASSIDY.	8TH N.S.
	F. T. CLAPHAM.	2/6TH R.WKS.
	T. COATES.	11TH YKS.
	J. COCKRILL.	12/13TH FUS.
	W. COLMER.	5TH D.L.I.
	J. CORNFORTH.	S. LANCS.
	B. CORR.	22ND LAB. CPS.
L/C.	I. COX.	6TH YKS.
PTE.	A. S. CROOKSTON.	16TH GORDON H.
BDR.	R. CROOKSTON.	R.G.A.
SCT.	F. CROSS.	R. FUS.
SPR.	C. R. CROZIER.	R.E.
STR.	H. DALRYMPLE.	R.N.R.
PTE.	J. W. DALRYMPLE.	YKS. REC.
	A. DAVIES.	5TH D.L.I.
	F. DAVIES.	K.O.S.B.
	W. H. DEE.	8TH N. FUS.
STR.	G. DENNISON. (M.M)	R.N.R.
C.R.A.	G. B. DOBBIN.	R.N.
PTE.	J. R. DONNISON.	2ND YKS.
	R. DUNN.	6TH GORDON H.
STR.	G. E. DUNNING.	R.N.
L/C.	A. DUNNING.	6TH YKS.
PTE.	W. DURKIN.	5TH YKS.

THESE ARE NAMES THAT MUST NOT WITHER.

The Racecourse

Racing at Thornaby began in 1724 on the Carrs which later became South Stockton's industrial belt. This forced racing to move to Mandale Marshes in 1855 but the name Stockton Races was retained. The four meetings a year were hugely popular and the main field also served for public gatherings such as the inauguration of the Borough and Royal visits.

Right, August 1922, major Thornaby landowner, The Fifth Earl of Harewood, Henry Lascelles, is seen on the left with Princess Mary, daughter of King George and Queen Mary whom he had married in Westminster Abbey in February.
The seventh Marquess of Londonderry on the right, 1878-1949 regularly hosted parties at Thornaby. Guests travelled by open landau with servants and provisions from Wynyard Park. Active in inter-war years government, Charles Vane-Tempest-Stewart later gained criticism for his appeasement views and contacts with leading Nazis during the 1930's, he met Adolf Hitler several times.

Below and right royalty and aristocracy are captured at Thornaby in August 1922 for society gossip magazines the Tatler and The Sketch.

WITH THEIR HOSTESS, THE MARCHIONESS OF LONDON-DERRY: PRINCESS MARY AND HER HUSBAND.

CHATTING TO LADY GISBOROUGH: THE MARQUESS OF ZETLAND.

LORD CASTLEREAGH, MR. CLAY AND L

VISCOUNT LASCELLES, PRINCESS MARY, AND THE MARQUESS OF LONDONDERRY

MARY FOX - STRANGWAYS,
ORDALE.

WITH LADY NUNBURNHOLME:
LORD STANLEY.

WITH MR. JACK LOWTHER:
LADY ZIA WERNHER.

My granddad took me to Stockton races from when I was about six in 1936 till he died in 1947 and every race week granddad picked me up and took me to the races. He had a saying: "If you're ever lucky don't forget to give a Beb to the bloke who brought you the luck, he'll be stood next to you." If you won 20 quid give someone a pound next to you, because he brought you the luck.

When it came to the war in 1939 there was only two courses in the North that stayed open, Pontefract and Stockton. They had alternate Saturdays, in addition Stockton's race week was in June for 3 days of racing, no matter where I was, we found our way to Stockton races.

The atmosphere was electric and Stockton was always crowded, coming down Brewery Bank and walking down the Wilderness road you couldn't get a bus to drive down there because the road was so full of people coming towards the race track and when it was over they all walked back again, some of them to Stockton, some of them to Thornaby, it was really popular. It was one of the best tracks in the country and I've raced all over the place. It was one of the top 3 courses in the North . There was two stands, the ten bob and the pound , Tattersalls and the Silver Ring , Tattersalls was right opposite the winning post and the Silver Ring about half a furlong from the winning post.

The stables were down at the end of Mandale Road they used to stable the horses there over night and take them back to the training ground. There was a load of litter after the racing and the women from the Erimus streets used to go out in big groups and pick up all the litter and got so much money for picking it up, that was a regular job.

People used to come in bus loads into Stockton Market have a few pints in the many pubs in Stockton High street and then go to the races, they used to come from Newcastle all over the place because it was the only track open on a Saturday . If you wanted a bet you had to do it on the course there was no betting shops before 1961 but there was a lot of back street betting. They were all over the place, the Police raided them now and then and kept them under control but it still went on.

You had tipsters, Prince Monolulu came to Stockton several times he used to have feathers in his hair. It was a social occasion you met your family there, you met friends, you'd ask them if they'd had a winner, you talked about horses and what you were going to do next and get a tip.

When they couldn't make any more money out of it they talked about putting houses on the site . Mandale bottoms used to flood then they altered the alignment of the river and it stopped. That's why it had such good grass because of the water. It was a good running track. I knew loads of people who worked there, there was a whole gang of waitresses who used to service the racecourses and they all lived in Thornaby, I met them in York, I met them in Ripon. They were just casual workers but they travelled together and that made it. They were lovely dressed, they had aprons with frilly bits , they had cuffs, they were proper waitresses and this gave it character. Then they disappeared and no one was eating meals there, it became a ham sandwich and burger joint. For years there was no money spent on the course and it just got run down, like the town hall, in the end they got a better offer from the retail people to turn it into Teesside Park. I hated it when I saw that grass being turned over.
ERIC SPAVIN

A summer meeting in the early 1960's, before the course changed it's name to Teesside Park in 1968. Held at Easter, Whitsun, July, August and October each year, meetings came to an end in 1981 when the course was cleared to build the Teesside Park retail complex.

Women from the Erimus community which was directly opposite the racecourse were employed to gather race cards and litter after the meetings. The group from right: Elizabeth Pemberton, Mrs Wood, Mrs Asco, Mrs Hartley, Florry Heads, Mabel Sharp, Reby Sharp, Lizzie Hood. About 1962.

The Londonderry party carriages climb Brewery Bank on their return to Wynyard Park after a race meeting in about 1910. Local pubs and hotels such as the Harewood Arms, right thrived with custom. In the previous century 36,000 visitors were once recorded over a three day meeting. Reactions to the party seem to reveal examples of class hostility rather than traditional deference.

The Great Depression

World recession affected Thornaby more seriously than many other towns. By the time this photograph was taken in the early 1930's Thornaby had endured seven years of mass unemployment. Significantly The Salvation Army featured here were well respected for providing much needed soup kitchens for the poor. Richardson Duck shipyard closed in 1923 with 300 redundancies, Whitwell's Iron Works had gone bankrupt in 1922 laying off 400 men, Thornaby's Craig Taylor shipyard closed in 1931 making another 400 redundant, while main employer Head Wrightson

A traditional Salvation Army Sunday gathering at the Five Lamps about 1930. The mood of the crowd appears sombre. Centre is Blooms one of three busy pawnshops, next door on the corner of Barnard Street a business is closing down.

was on short time due to lack of orders. The effects of the ensuing poverty on children in particular was visible in the streets of the town, mortality rates increased dramatically. Thornaby Council fought the County authority and government unsuccessfully to introduce free school meals and free school milk to help prevent malnutrition. It wasn't until the policies of the 1945 Labour Government and the efforts of crusading MP's like Ellen Wilkinson that free milk and free meals were introduced fully in Thornaby Schools.

AZETTE, WEDNESDAY,

DERELICT SHIPYARDS

MACHINERY SOLD AT BARGAIN PRICES

£800 LOT FOR £17

THE sale by public auction of the three Tees shipyards (Messrs Craig, Taylor, and Company, Thornaby; Messrs

Right, a redundancy letter 1931. Above, 1932 and the assets of the dismantled Thornaby shipyards prove to be virtually worthless. The yards had re-invested in new equipment after the war expecting an upturn in orders.

CRAIG, TAYLOR & Co. LTD.
SHIPBUILDERS & ENGINEERS

Telegrams
CRATAYLOR
STOCKTON·ON·TEES.

Telephones
636 (Three lines)

Codes
A.B.C. 5th Edition

STOCKTON - ON - TEES

To........Mr. H. Gladders........   3rd June, 1931.

Dear Sir

We exceedingly regret that owing to the continued depression in the Industry, we are reluctantly compelled to close down the Shipyard.

You may rest assured that the Directors have only decided to take this step after very long and careful consideration

I remember 1930 Head Wrightson's fabrication shops were empty, there wasn't a job in. All the men were finished. One yard manager was kept on and the apprentices were kept on week on and week off. At sixteen year old I was drawing dole, little bit it was, it wasn't much, but that's how it was. And we went like that until 1935 when things began to get a little bit better.

In 1930 one of the curates in Thornaby went round the butchers every Friday and Saturday night and got all the bones he could get, he had a witches brew, and he set that up in Trafalgar Street, with a fire underneath and made some soup. And there was a queue of people with Billy cans who came along, that was their meal that day. And that's the sort of spirit, they took all that. There was no money in Thornaby, absolutely none at all, it was a poor town but it was a proud town.   MAYNARD WILSON

CHILDREN STARVING AT THORNABY

FAMILIES LIVING ON 2.36D PER MEAL

COUNCIL'S ALARM

"DAMNING INDICTMENT OF MEANS TEST"

The cruelty of the authorities and in particular the Means Test made regular news in early 1930's Thornaby. Right, men queue for the Dole at an unidentified Labour Exchange.

An emotional Council meeting was reported in the Stockton and Tees-side Herald on 13th May 1933: Mayor Councillor Brennan commented "Anyone with eyes can see deterioration after years of unemployment. It is impossible to have anything else than deterioration with only 2.36d per meal. " How any Government in a Christian country can allow a state of affairs like this to continue is beyond me." he added. Councillor Dacre, who moved that the resolution be sent to the county authority said that they would be lacking in their duties as public representatives unless they made another attempt to get something done for the starving school children of Thornaby . The death rate in Thornaby was 3.92 whereas today it was 12.65, which showed that not only were people starving, but that they were dying owing to an abominable means test.

One day I was late for school and was lined up with others to take my punishment which was one stroke of the cane. Standing next to me was a boy from a very poor family, and as we stood with heads bowed while the tirade from the headmistress fell about our ears. I saw that he didn't have any shoes on his feet, nothing at all on his bare feet. Knowing this lad had walked all the way to school from Below the Railway I began to cry. Later there was a charity called the Mayor's Boot Fund which provided one pair of boots for each needy family, forms were given out in schools then you were given a chit to take to the Co-op in Stockton or Greenlees in Mandale Road . Inside the boots were marked Mayor's Boot Fund and not allowed to be accepted by pawnbrokers.

The degradation of the hated Means Test meant that a great number of families lived below the poverty line in what was to prove a vicious circle. There were frequent visits from Government inspectors, who if they saw anything of value in your home such as a wireless set, gramophone or even a nice piece of furniture would consider that you could sell these items and therefore you were not in need and again your allowance would be cut. A man was allowed about 15 shillings for himself and about ten shillings for his wife weekly, in social benefits and about one shilling per head for each child. As children grew older and left school they might find employment and subsequently had to move away to another part of the country to work on farms or the Yorkshire mills, anyone bringing in to a family any extra income would find they were no better off because this would be deducted from what the father had been paid.

Pat's father Michael Gilgallon in Royal Marine uniform. For many Thornaby people who served their country during the war the return could be another battle - the search for work.

When I was 14 I had to go away to work to Bingley, I used to get paid once a month and I used to send money home. That was the only way I could support my family. Dad used to meet me at the station to carry my case .The last time I came he wasn't there, mam said "Oh he's got a job digging air raid shelters" And I went to Robert Street near to the Town Hall to see him and he was in this big hole and I remember saying " Aw dad you're too old for that. " "Oh It's a job lass, it's a job." That was the first job he'd had since the early 1930's. But he died in the November of 1939, too much for him probably. He had pernicious Anaemia, there was no cure for it then. He just went down and down, he just died in his sleep. It was disastrous, you love your dad, I did. PAT STOKES (GILGALLON)

Tommy Thompson, manager of Blooms pawn shop taken in 1971 before it closed. Blooms was one of three busy pawnbrokers. Clothing could be pledged, behind Tommy lie stacks of unclaimed suits.

Before Dad could get any work he had the Means Test people come round to see if we had anything we could sell before they gave you any assistance, a rug or some lino even so you had to sell that, it was horrendous. It was like the boot club, a charity set up to provide boots for children who were going barefoot, sometimes you were too proud to go to the boot club but it was there.

Me mother used to take Dad's medals to the pawnshop if there was no buffs meeting he didn't need them. He had all the paraphernalia, he was in the Royal Antediluvian Order of Buffaloes(the Buffs) This day he came in and said "There's a big raising at the buffs tonight." (An Exaltation) Well Gertie nearly dropped ! " Here you go and see Gerry who had the pawnshop, go round and ask Gerry if I can have your dad's medals out and I'll bring them straight back tomorrow and pay him the interest." And he did. But lots of people went, nobody had any money to lend you, no one would lend you anything so you had to go to the pawnshop. GLADYS GODWIN (FULTON)

Josie Bayles is an example of the important role Thornaby women played in the war effort. Seen here on the left with a colleague, Josie volunteered to be a female porter at Thornaby Station, her tasks involved heavy work that included uncoupling carriages.

The War in Thornaby 1939-1945

Thornaby made a huge contribution to the national war effort and at works like Head Wrightson a strong team spirit emerged to complete the punishing schedules of war production. The overall Head Wrightson workforce expanded from 3000 to 5500 including 1000 women, not seen in any pre war factories, and who trained as skilled welders and drillers to replace the 1000 men called up, most women passed their training as welders in just ten weeks. Head Wrightson quickly converted shops for war production and supplied a range of key equipment some of it specialist: this included Bailey Bridges, aircraft hangers, tank tracks and underground shelters. Many working people volunteered for duties such as air raid wardens, the home guard, and the Fire Service.

Right, the launch of landing craft LCG 177 on November 17th, 1944, the 201st ship to be constructed. The Stockton Construction Company, a Tees consortium made sections of each craft which were then put together by Head Wrightson. The derelict slipways of Richardson Duck's shipyard last used in 1921 were brought back to life to launch the landing crafts.

William Callaghan, shipwright was awarded the British Empire Medal in 1945 and he is symbolic of the major contribution Thornaby people made to war production. At Head Wrightson since boyhood Mr Callaghan supervised the construction of over 200 landing craft and other ships at a rate of eight a month. He is seen here on the right with a colleague, behind them a craft ready to be launched on November 17th 1944. A total of 238 ships were built at Thornaby during the war.

Right, a 1942 German reconnaissance photo of Head Wrightson works printed in a company brochure, the main centres of production have been marked up. Above, the Easter 1941 attack by a parachute bomb at Head Wrightson's Teesdale Works caused serious damage to the mine shop, where bomb casings were produced. Fortunately most of the work force was still on Easter holiday. Work resumed in a few days.

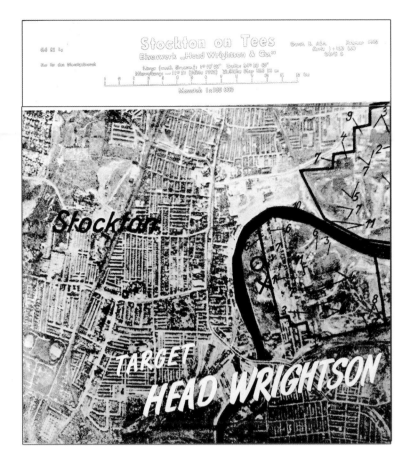

We took the jobs of the men who'd gone off to fight. You were conscripted there, either that or the army. So my dad said "you're not going in the army you're going to Head Wrightson they want you there, we'll look after you for your own sake." We learned from the men, and I could go back now and do all those jobs, you did so many different jobs. We just accepted what it was all about, you knew you were doing your bit for the war. We couldn't get home fast enough to go to the dance, at the Maison de Dance or the Jubilee Hall till ten o clock at night then you were up at next morning to go to work, six till two then night shifts.

I met my husband at work, I had been going in doing night shift, I used to meet him coming out of work as I was going in, I wasn't the only one in that position other women had the same. I don't know how we had time to get married. It was very very black on a night, he used to whistle a tune, <u>La Paloma</u>, and he whistled that and I knew where he was stood. You couldn't see a hand in front of you. Even your bikes had a little tiny hole in the lamp itself. I used to do the home guard as well, if you were free for night time, "Right you're on tonight." Tin hat the lot, I was in the air raid shelter and they were all singing, then there was a hell of a bang. The head chief said "You are wanted Connie up behind the town hall some houses have been bombed." And when I went up it was my sister, she was living with her mother in law. It was her house and she came out covered in muck and dust with a baby three month old in her arms. She was underneath the stairs, that's what saved her. It was very hush hush though you never knew what went on. CONNIE WASS (TUNNEY)

It was terrible, absolutely terrible really I don't want to think about it. We were sheltering in the cellar, where we went every night, my brother pushed us in there. If it hadn't been for my brother Hubert we would have all been killed. Because he turned his boat upside down against the window and it shielded us from the blast and Dad reinforced the cellar in every way he could and it worked, he was a good joiner. We were in there when the police found us, the people in the street were looking for us wondering where we were. A policeman picked me up, I was 11 years old and said "We've been looking for you all night." We had nowhere to go so they took us down to a hall in Trafalgar Street. I went with a girl called Winnie Bolt, the same age as me, she gave me a bed for the night in her room and I've always wanted to find her and thank her for the kindness she showed us. Dad said the worst night of his life was when we were bombed, he was at work on night shift and came home to find the roads cordoned off. One bomb went into the mud bank and didn't go off, we didn't hear any more of it for years after and then someone found it. It was on the front page of the news, "Bomb Found." It had to be de-fused. We were lucky. CATHERINE LUCK (SANDERSON)

Left, Thornaby Place, left, where Catherine Luck lived, photographed during the 1950's.

We had the aerodrome at the top of the road and we watched the searchlights picking out the planes. We knew as kids which was a German plane, you could tell from the sound it was different, you could hear, the Dornier bombers were more of a rumble. We were scared but not as scared as the kids in London must have been. For part of the war I slept with Mrs Leeson, Auntie Florrie who lived across the road because she was deaf. I had to wake her up when the siren went and then open the door for my family across the road to come through her kitchen through the yard into the shelter in the back street.
MARY HUDSON (HAYCOCK)

The council came round and said there are young men 17 to 18 who didn't have accommodation on the airfield so they have to lodge with us two at a time in the other bedroom. I remember one couple, his mother wrote and thanked my mam, his sister used to send me her old dresses which you didn't get in the war. I remember the fear of the sirens especially with these young men going off from the airfield and them not coming back, you didn't know where they went. We had a Canadian pilot he was killed over Scotland. I remember mam saying. " I lent him a case and now we'll never get it back."We didn't know where my dad was or where my uncles were they were all in the services, eventually we found out dad was in the far east.
PAULINE NICHOL

We were bombed out. The sirens had gone one night and we had the all clear. We got back into the house when the sirens went again, my mother got me Betty and Harry out to the air raid shelter and she left my dad in the house to bring our John out. My father had one speed, dead slow. So we got over to the shelter and we hadn't been in long when the bomb dropped, another split-second and it would have hit the air raid shelter, it hit the railway line. We honestly thought we'd have no house to come out to, but by this time father hadn't turned up. My dad had laid our John down on the settee just before the bomb dropped, then when it dropped the blast blew the back door off and it covered our John so all the glass fell onto the floor fortunately. That door had saved our John from getting cut to ribbons, he was dead dead lucky. We had to go to the rest centre then because all our houses at the bottom half of George Street weren't fit to live in there was no windows in them. The air raid warden was killed and there was Mr Hornsby who was killed in the Britannia Pub just a few streets away from us, he stayed in bed that night and the blast killed him, it was disastrous.
WINNIE MCHUGH (BIGGINS)

Thornaby's aerodrome and it's concentration of industry were both magnets for raids but the town was bombed relatively lightly compared to the London Blitz and the later devastating V1 and V2 rocket attacks in the capital. Altogether five Thornaby residents were killed during the air raids and 38 seriously injured, hundreds of homes were damaged. The worst raid, of 11 March 1943 killed three people, Robert Hornsby, James Lambert and an on duty air raid warden Mrs Miriam Pugh. 72 people were injured and 550 were made homeless.

Homes in front of Pumphrey's sugar factory on Stephenson Street damaged in the 1943 raid, feature on the cover of a book published by the company at the end of the war .

The medical volunteers who attended civilian air raids. On the left of Dr McKay centre, is team leader Florence Spence who trained at Stockton and Thornaby hospital during the first war. Back row, the Civil Defence volunteers who provided medical assistance and who were tasked with removing the injured and any bodies from the scene. The nurses duties extended to day to day demands at the George Street Welfare Centre where they were based.

This group of Wireless Operators and Air Gunners in front of an Avro Anson in 1939 reveals the wartime sacrifices young people made: only three of these men survived. Left to right: Vic Gent was killed in July 1940 when his Hudson aircraft hit cables at Boldon, T. Bayfield survived, Ted Pritchard was missing off Hartlepool in December 1940, Jock Stirling survived, Ronald Mew was transferred to Bomber Command and killed in 1941 in an accident, Bill Parfitt was killed at Ingleby Arncliffe, January 1944, K. Maddocks was shot down off Norway in April 1940, Jack Sheeky survived the war and married a local woman.

Aerodrome 1929-1945

Thornaby began as an auxiliary aerodrome of mainly part timers in 1929 and when war broke out it was launched into full time service. The resident 608 Squadron had a range of training tasks during the 1930's, in wartime it's fleets of Hudson and Anson aircraft performed essential roles in the defence of the country as part of Coastal Command. They were joined by the regular Squadron 220 at the start of the war. Known affectionately as the Kipper Patrol, 608 had a range of key duties on the North Sea such as searches for possible German invasion forces, anti submarine patrols, convoy escorts, air sea rescue missions and reconnaissance. Coastal Command was a sort of CID of the North Sea and sought out whatever the enemy was up to. The aerodrome had a major impact on the local economy and remained a valuable source of jobs and skills.

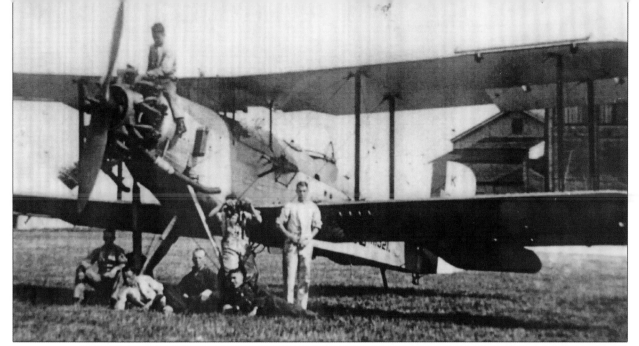

Snapshots taken in 1936 by engineer Robert Thomson who made a fine record of the aerodrome's early years with his camera. Robert left a country croft in Aberdeenshire and had no idea of his Thornaby destination when he enrolled in the RAF but spent most of the rest of his life in the town after marrying Josie Bayles (page 97). Wartime service led him to photograph adventures in Egypt, The Sudan and South Africa.

The airfield complex about 1936 just after construction. Millbank Lane is on the far left and bottom left The Oddfellow's Arms. No main runways were built at this point and as war approached the plane sheds were supplemented by the distinctive "C" Type hanger.

A Hudson crew return to Thornaby after a flight over the North Sea. They each carry important items for wartime operations: Air Gunner LAC Bayfield holds a reconnaissance camera, Wireless Operator LAC Darbyshire a pigeon basket. (Homing pigeons were successful in carrying distress messages from sea ditched crews.) Pilot Sergeants Sposton and Arnott carry their parachutes.

Wartime Hudsons from 608 Squadron over Yorkshire in 1941. Spitfires and Blenheims were also on hand to protect convoys from attack.

In Februrary 1940 three Hudson aircraft from 220 Squadron at Thornaby on a reconnaissance mission located the German prison ship the Altmark off the Norwegian coast and it was shadowed until intercepted by the Royal Navy resulting in the freeing of 299 allied prisoners of war.

During the war hundreds of airmen and WAAFS were stationed at Thornaby. The aerodrome was an important source of employment and work skills for the town, enabling local people to learn from regular personnel. Many of the servicemen and ground crew were from the area.

Victory's Children

On May 8th 1945, children sat down to VE Day parties like this one all over Britain to celebrate the end of the war. But this group in Barnard Street is special not only because it is such a well composed photograph but because after research everyone in it could be identified. Further work led to finding nearly all the survivors and the siblings of the deceased for interviews to discover what the intervening years had brought them. The gathering embodies an intricate web of kinship and community and studies revealed that for these young people the common bonds of community and street was important to their identity and development as individuals. Outside the frame the parents are at work building the new Britain in the long journey from austerity to relative prosperity. Barnard Street is now long gone, buried under the A66 dual carriageway in the early 1980's but these testimonies and photographs remain to give us a glimpse of each of these children's futures.

Everybody came out and after the party they lit a bonfire in the middle of the street and brought music on. Harry Fulton dragged a piano out of the house and played it in the street, people were dancing, it was marvellous. Everybody came out, all the neighbours and all the kids roasted potatoes in the fire. The adults were totally relieved the war was over.   EILEEN HENDERSON (HAYCOCK)

Left, V.E. Day party, Barnard Street May 8th 1945.

Ken Morrison 1942-

I always liked mechanical things so I knew I would be going in to something working with my hands. If you think of the schooling we got we were trained up to be practical. Arthur Head had proper blacksmiths shops for us to use and also joiners shops and we were producing reasonable standard metalwork and carpentry work even at an early age. So we were set on the tracks for getting an apprenticeship when we got to school leaving age. I started at Ashmores who paid for all the further education for us and we got one day off a week for six years to do all the different courses, so I ended up with a decent qualification that took me on to the next level. During my life I've been taking more and more courses and exams. I finished up as a Quality Assurance manager for a Swiss company building refineries.

Ray Costello 1942-1996

Ray was the eldest of the family he had to look after me there was hell to pay if he didn't. My mother always had aspirations for us but neither of us aspired to be anything other than what we were, we had no great designs on being doctors or solicitors or anything of that nature, we just grew up as part of life and went to school as best as possible. We weren't particularly over endowed with education to the extent that we could become doctors or solicitors, we were just normal lads growing up and went to school and did our best, we left school and got a job that was suitable at the time. Since then we raised families and made the best life we could. I think Ray was fulfilled with his life and work and he never had a day off until his illness. I wouldn't turn the clock back to see if there was anything I could change and have done different, my brother Ray was quite content with his lot as I am with mine now, that's the way it was.
FRED COSTELLO

Fishing on the Tees 1970's

Gladys Godwin (Fulton) 1938-2012

The photograph of us was taken in 1957, we'd been to the fair on the Bon Lea field on a Friday or Saturday night. I was home on leave from the RAF, we'd been courting only six months, we'd met at Paleschi's coffee shop a famous meeting place in the town where a lot of married couples met and were married 12 months later, we just liked each other and decided to get married. We had our ups and downs like everybody did but we were very happy. When I left the Air Force Gladys worked with us in our furniture shop on Norton Road called Affordable Furniture. And that's what we did, our customers were from the poorer parts of town and we offered decent three piece suites and such at a price people could afford. We were like a working team. We made a living and it all went well until Gladys got to be 67 when trade was altering and we decided we'd had enough so we sold the property and retired. We had 28 years of a living, not a fantastic living but we had no reason to complain, all the children had nice weddings. We used to work it as a family concern. We have three sons and one daughter and ten grandchildren so we had 54 years of happy married life. This is an unusual picture, because ordinary people didn't have cameras in those days so most photographs were treasured, like I treasure this one. Gladys took a copy of this picture to her grave and a copy will go with me when I die. HENRY GODWIN

Gladys and Henry at a fair on the Bon Lea field 1957.

A reverse view of Barnard Street from the party table ten years later in 1955 looking towards George Street. Gladys Fulton's mother Gladys senior walks by seven Barnard Street, behind her is the Haycock family house, in front is Toni Paleschi's home at nine Barnard Street. Eleven, just visible is brother in law Howard Fulton's house. Nine Barnard Street became Gladys and Henry's home soon after they were married.

Beryl Story (Scott) 1936 -

I worked at Payton and Baldwins till I got married in 1959. Vic was a sheet metal worker, electric welder at Wilkinsons near the station and he was offered a house in Derwent Road by a chap he worked with for £2000. We used to go to the pictures three times a week then, once to the Mayfair and twice to the Queens, "we'll knock off spending" all those sweets and we both used to smoke, ice cream and everything so we'd save up our £300 deposit. The mortgage was ten pound a month which was what Vick's wages was per week. We might have settled for a little terrace house but we saved up and saved up, we said we'll wait another year and we got the semi detached house in Derwent Road. My mam thought that was lovely "Our Beryl's got a house in Derwent Road." The family were all pleased we'd done well. Vic died in 1976 of cancer at the age of 37, Caroline was 12 Craig was 14 and I had to have more income and I applied for a job at the Doctor's surgery and got it, the doctors were very nice. It got to the stage when people would ring up and they'd say "Hello Beryl" they got to know my voice, I was there till I retired, it was lovely.

Eileen Henderson (Haycock) 1932-2017

There was a time when we had the school plays I was shy but I still played the major part in the play so there was a time up to my teens when I would have loved to be an actress, except in all the movies they were beautiful and I didn't think I was particularly attractive. My first job was in Head Wrightson in the office, many of the girls had it drummed in to them that their ambition should be to get married and have children because girls didn't do anything else then, there was no incentive. I think that probably disappeared a few years later in the 1960's when opportunities began to get better for girls. We've been here in America 39 years, I've been here as long as I've lived in England. Had my dad been alive I don't think I would have come, I adored him but he died in 1972. We came to the states in 1974, Graham came here a week to work then he sent for me. I don't like the cold so the warmth was attractive. Graham was a consultant design engineer, he had a good job. We bought this house with a huge garden it was lovely, the weather was gorgeous, we've had a good life in America especially in Texas. Here in Dallas neighbours don't mix at all you don't ever go out on the front and talk to each other there is no togetherness or neighbourliness like there was in Thornaby which is what I miss.

Mary Hudson (Haycock) 1928-

I just took off with 30 Bob in my pocket on the bus to London it was the worst fog you've ever seen. I met a girl on the bus she was an ex-WAFF I got some digs with her landlady's cousin and I got a job. You could get a job easily then. I got about three jobs then Cyril my partner moved down when he was 21 and I moved out to Welwyn Garden City, and we were very happy. When I first went to London I joined the Labour League of Youth, I can remember how inspirational they were fighting to get things done, I thought the creation of NHS was fantastic but that spirit has been lost now. I can remember the great speakers after the war, it was so inspiring. Atlee, the two Bevans: Bevin and Bevan they were all great. There's a lot of sentimentality about Barnard Street but it was tough, it was a hard life. I'm not sorry that I experienced it but given the choice I might have chosen a different sort of childhood but I had loving parents even though things went wrong at times.

Left, Vic Story at Derwent Road 1964.

Top Jack and Mary Haycock, London 1949. Left, Eileen and Mary with their mother Mary at the new council house in Hutton Close about 1960.

Raymond Fulton 1933-2003

I got a job down Head Wrightson in 1946 as a heater lad and later I served my time as a riveter at the Malleable, we did a 48 hour week including Saturday morning. There was a squad of us working together, a riveter, a holder up and a heater lad. We used to build rail wagons, we'd put six or seven hundred rivets on a wagon. I felt like turning round and running away at first, everything was that black and massive. Going to work as a 14 year old lad, it was bit tough especially going to work in the dark. It took a while to accept it all. Riveting was on the way out though, more tack welding was being done so I came to the end of serving my time after six years and they finished me. Once you were 21 they'd get someone else and pay them less. I got into the Head Wrightson steel mill, five at night to seven o clock the next morning on five or six pound a week for four shifts, that was often 50 hours. A lot of lads went to night school, a few years on I thought I wish I'd done that, but being a riveter was so straightforward. All I wanted to do early on was keep in a job and earn some money. In 1967 I moved across the river to Kennedy's who made steel flooring, we knew the money was there every week, you had a tough but steady job. I was there 27 years and retired in 1994 at 63. I've got my caravan at Saltburn so now I can enjoy myself at last. (Interviewed in 2001)

Bill Crone 1933-2009

Nearly all the family were involved in running shops in some way, his mother had the shop in Barnard Street which was a gold mine, she bought him a marvellous Jowett Javelin in the late 1950's and it was his pride and joy. We moved to the village of Greatham where his aunt Maud had the main shop, she was retiring so we took it over for 25 years and lived in a house attached to the shop as his mother had done in Barnard Street. Greatham village has kept it's community spirit and everyone gets together just like they did in Barnard Street. Bill also did very well as a heating engineer and he had his own business installing central heating systems. We went on a lot of holidays, he loved heat, we could never go anywhere where there was snow, he used to like to get heat on his body during the winter months to last for the rest of the year. We went on Med cruises, the Bahamas, Barbados and Cyprus. He was a lovely person, I don't think he had a bad word about anybody, he was the loveliest person he wouldn't argue with anyone I don't think we ever had an argument.
YVONNE CRONE

Dorothy Toulson (Crone) 1930-2018

I was only eight when we came back to Thornaby from Blue Hall estate, mam brought us over to Thornaby one night along New Street, there was gas lit streets in the rain and I thought it was the Black Hole of Calcutta. She was going to open a shop and all I can remember was my mother having no money at all. We were terrified when the air raid sirens went during the war, I can understand how with all the anxiety mam came to have a duodenal ulcer later on in life, coping with the business and everything else. Everybody was really happy the day of the photograph, there was a relief and joy at knowing you'd never hear a siren again, that's what's behind that photograph of us all in Barnard Street. Later when I was in the prime of my life I thought I'd had a beautiful life and I still think that. Norman always earned a decent wage and we've always had a car, he retired at 60 luckily we were in a pension and if he wasn't here I'd get it, everything has been an experience.

The shop Helen Crone, Dorothy's mother opened up in 1939 on the corner of Barnard Street and Queen Street.

Raymond Fulton returns home after Sunday morning overtime at Kennedy's foundry, 1972.

Toni Paleschi 1935-1999

Our family came from Italy, my granddad Dominic started the well known ice cream shop by the five lamps and began to make his own ice cream. Toni my brother and I were all part of the business. The work ethic was very much an Italian thing and everyone in the family worked, it was all family orientated. This all went back to the 1930's and before. It was all quite disciplined as well but the community was very close in Barnard Street. I was the youngest so had it a bit easier but Toni along with his cousin Albert used to be down at the factory behind Barnard Street crack of dawn every morning in the 1950's preparing the van. They also had to bring in the blocks of ice delivered at the end of the backstreet, and drag them down the alley, it was hard work. In Toni's day the business wasn't that big so he went into being an electrician, he did an apprenticeship at Head Wrightson but he still used to go out on a weekend for my father in the ice cream van, dad was notorious for getting us all to work. Toni started working for Stockton Council but he'd always been involved in the business when father went on holiday he would be left behind and ran the business. He was a nice man. VINCENT PALESCHI

Ronald Scott 1930-2008

Ron my brother left school at 15 he always wanted to play the piano, he tap danced as well and the lino used to be worn out where he had practiced. My dad said he had to serve his time, he had to have a trade so he started work at Head Wrightson as a fitter and turner. He lasted only a couple of weeks and said I'm not doing this any more. And he went off to London to be a musician. He tap danced, he taught himself to play the piano, he could play the violin. In the RAF he joined one of the bands and played the trumpet. He played in bands in the 1950's and 60's starting round about the time of Victor Sylvester. Ronnie became Sam Scott the entertainer and his talents led him to dance, sing and do comedy routines in South Africa, Germany, Australia and the USA. He took northern humour with him around the globe, Ron even recreated a Thornaby pub in Bangcock which he ran, it was quite successful. He always sent my mam a cheque every month, and he wrote to her every week. He met an American woman from Philadelphia and ended up living there where he eventually trained as a nurse in order to care for her since she later developed cancer. BERYL STORY

Jack Haycock 1932-2004

Jack Haycock became a sheet metal worker after a spell in the navy during the early 1950's and did his apprenticeship at Aerex Fans, Stockton where he learned high quality metalwork. Father John Haycock also worked here as the company buyer, and he later set up his own metalwork company employing members of the family including Jack. The photograph shows Jack as an apprentice in 1947 to his left is Norman Toulson who met Dorothy Crone on a visit to Barnard Street and later married her.

Toni Paleschi with partner Barbara out on the road with the family ice cream van during the 1960's

Ronald Scott set up a successful attraction in Bangcock called the Yard of Ale, based on a Thornaby pub.

116

David Green 1942 -

I did try to get into Head Wrightson's with some friends and we went down. A job was a job then but when my father found out he said "No you're not coming in here, If I catch you in here there'll be trouble." Head Wrightson killed him in a way, all the fumes, the muck and dust plus the cigarettes although he did give up the smoking. When he did pass away and they opened him up they said his lungs were full of dust, a lifetime in the foundry, so I'm glad he got me out of it because he was 63 when he died which was no age. I went for an interview and then got a start as an apprentice joiner for six years, then I worked in the shipyards onshore modules, fitting them out. I have always been the gypsy and later worked all over, Iran, Holland, Germany. At the time there wasn't the work in Britain and the money was very poor compared to what we were getting over there in Germany. I lived in Holland for 25- 30 years and when I retired I bought a nice big house with a nice big garden in a village in Germany. The neighbours are half Dutch and half German, we're on the border. The people are fantastic there's no animosity, nothing. My neighbours are my age or older and they hate talking about the war. I have no regrets working and traveling in the way I did, I've seen so many amazing places.

Kathleen Alder (Haycock)1942-

That's myself at the front next to my cousin David, my brother Jacky is further down, on the opposite side is my sister Eileen and stood up is my sister Mary. I can't remember this day at all but my memories of Barnard Street are rich, even though I left at ten or eleven I have stronger memories of Barnard Street than anywhere else I've lived. We all knew each other we knew everybody who lived in every house, there was Catholics, Protestants, Presbyterians and salvationists but I can't remember anyone falling out over religion. We just all got along so well together a very close community. It's a bit like where I live now on the Green, people look out for each other. From the Barnard Street years till now I don't think you'll ever see the jump again that's been from then to these days, I don't think it's necessarily a good thing either I think we've grown far too materialistic including myself and some how we've lost some kind of spirit, some kind of caring. There's also a lot more debt now. I know people who've come from Cannon Street and Thornaby and done OK and my children have done OK, but there's a lot that haven't. They rely on their parents to help them out, then we all had jobs, strangely enough the opportunities seemed greater then.

Rita Wilson 1930-

Rita married Norman Wood from Billingham in 1956 and they began their life together in the family home at number 1A Barnard Street where their first child Karen was born. They family moved to a house in Billingham in 1957, Norman died in 1986 but Rita continues to live in Billingham.

Above, Rita's sister Ann outside the family home at 1A Barnard Street in about 1962.

David Green in his garden at Bad Bentheim on the German, Dutch border 2012.

Kathleen Alder (right) with sister Mary at the wedding of Kathleen's son at Crathorne Hall 2012.

An Air Sea Rescue Avro Lancaster with 279 squadron on the Thornaby runway in November 1945. 279 had been transferred to Thornaby in 1944 and was disbanded in 1946.

VE Day party May 1945 in the drill hall, local residents celebrate the end of hostilities in Europe with squadron personnel. Thornaby aerodrome was part of the community and relatively accessible. However proximity to residential areas prevented the site from developing due to safety concerns.

Aerodrome 1945-1957

Developing Cold War concerns in Post War Britain brought new roles, including in 1948 The 3608 (North Riding) Fighter Control Unit which trained men and women as Radar Operators and Fighter Plotters.

So vital are these Units to our defences it would be no exaggeration to say that successful repulsion of an air attack in the event of war would depend entirely on adequate manning with skilled personnel. Air Ministry leaflet.

My encounter with planes began dramatically in 1941 when me and my mother were crossing Victoria Bridge from Stockton and a gunner in a German plane shot at us as we headed for Mandale Road where we lived. We were very lucky neither of us were hit, but it was terrifying. I left the Boys Brigade and joined 1261 Thornaby Air Cadets. Then a job came up and I started work on the station in 1955 as a civy in charge of mail so I got to know everyone, I ended up being one of the last people to work there. 608 Squadron was mainly weekend airmen in those days, but we had three regular airmen who didn't have a day job, Hancock, Joyce and Mackenzie and they were the 608 regular airmen. Monday to Friday they used to book in and get their flying hours in that's why 608 Squadron was top of the list for the amount of hours flown. They were qualified pilots but they were auxiliaries so they were knick named the regular auxiliaries. We used to get a lot of flying in either a Sycamore Helicopters or the back seat of a Meteor. On a weekend, once or twice a month we had target practice, a Meteor used to trail a big drogue behind it, a large piece of fabric and they'd take it over the north sea and the other Vampires would fire at it with coloured shells so they would leave an impression and give you your score mark. The local economy did well from the station especially the Oddfellows pub. Upstairs there was the cocktail bar and that was affectionately known as the officer's mess, all the ranks were downstairs in the bars.

Nothing was that different from wartime, the aircraft were serviced by instrument fitters and engine fitters they'd strip down the engine and put it back together again and give it a full throttle to see if everything was OK. One day the Squadron Leader's wife was on the airfield with her poodle and the dog wasn't on a lead and it ran behind this Vampire that was on full throttle, the force lifted this poodle off the deck into the air and it came down with a wallop, it yelped but was non the worse for wear thankfully . The chief said " You shouldn't be here when we're doing engine run ups, it's dangerous."

When you went to Summer Camp for a week there used to be 600 or 700 cadets, you'd stay under canvas or in the H Blocks. Our last camp was 1956 because we thought we were all going to be called up for Suez. When on the 5th and 4th November the Suez crisis blew up, there was this call up rumour. We'd just come back from camp in Gibraltar, but nothing happened at Thornaby. Then all of a sudden the government announced it was closing all of the auxiliary squadrons.

Then in 1965 we moved into a house on the airfield estate right opposite the old hangers at 83 Millbank Lane. The tower blocks nearby were named Hudson and Anson House in memory of the main serving aircraft at Thornaby. The houses were all built to Parker-Morris standards, they were lovely houses there's no doubt about it and 83 Millbank looked right over to the old hangers where I used to give the cadets foot drill as squadron warrant officer. ALAN HUITSON

The No. 275 Search and Rescue Squadron set up at Thornaby in 1954, this was the only helicopter SAR unit in the RAF at the time and on 24 hour stand by. The helicopter was able to get airborne within ten minutes of receiving an emergency call. The squadron used Bristol Sycamore helicopters like the one in this staged photograph.

Air displays were popular events attracting enthusiastic crowds, it was a chance for the RAF to show off it's latest jet aircraft such as this Gloster Javelin. Below, the final show in 1957.

Most aircraft were jet propelled and technically complex which meant the level of expertise increased beyond the scope of many auxiliary part timers. Also major defence cuts and a review of defence policy after the 1956 Suez conflict led to all 21 of the Auxiliary Squadrons being closed down. In 1957 608 was disbanded. By October 1958 the RAF had left the site which the Air Ministry eventually sold in 1962 to Thornaby Town Council, providing land for the creation of the New Town and much needed housing.

The Cruel Winter

My dad tells a story about the dreadful winter of 1947. They'd all been drinking in Batty's pub and this young man came in, he was very upset, his wife was dying of pneumonia. He had no money, he'd burned everything you could burn, they had no coal, they had nothing. "Does someone have coal that they can let me have? "But everybody was in the same state. Someone said: "There's all that coal in the Co op coal sheds." Which was just round the corner in Wedgewood Street, " If only we could get to that." My dad knew a way of getting in beyond the locks when he was a kid. Dad had just come back from India and Burma and he had lost so much weight he'd spent his war years out there and he was very very thin. "I bet I could still find my way into there." So the whole group of gentlemen, maybe they'd had a little bit too much to drink, staggered round to the coal sheds in Wedgewood Street. Sure enough dad could still remember how to get beyond the gates, and he got in and opened the gates. They started off with the young man who'd first asked for help and a sack of coal was taken to his house Then as many of the old folks that they could think of they took sacks of coal to them, and anyone who was ill they could think of in this small community, they all got a sack of coal. It's just evidence of the community as it was then. Granted it wasn't quite legal but perhaps it was morally correct that it saved old people, probably from dying.
CHRISTINE LYMER (DANKS)

Jimmy Danks, above, in India during World War two. Below, Jimmy had been born next door to The Prince of Wales pub or Batty's as it was affectionately known and spent most of his life in the area around Hope Street. Part of the Co-op coal yard can be seen on the left on Wedgewood Street.

Holidays With Pay

I said to my sister, I'll tell you what I've just been reading the paper where you can book a plane. I always read the small print. So I wrote up to the firm, it was an RAF bi plane, a de Havilland Rapide. It cost me £35 to book the plane to take five of us to the Isle of Man and back. They were in Newcastle so I said "We've got an airfield in our own town." so they said "For a ten shilling note we'll pick you up, we'll come down and pick you up. " We had a pilot and a co pilot. Our first week's holiday on pay, there was five of us, a lad out of the fleet air arm, my sister and my husband to be and another young man who'd just lost his wife through childbirth We had a week there, coming back though there was an electric storm and the plane couldn't take off so they said sorry we have to stay the night. We found a haystack in a nearby field and we pulled out places to sleep in cubby holes for the night. But we didn't turn up that night. We said we're stuck in the airport at Peel, we weren't allowed up in the electric storm. Could you believe it ? 1948 was the first holidays from Head Wrightson with pay, you used to get holidays with no pay. It was marvellous.

CONNIE WASS (TUNNEY)

Right, Richard Wass was a fitter and turner at Head Wrightson where the couple met, below Connie with work colleague at Head Wrightson.

A family business

George Hall in about 1938 with one of the coal delivery horses stabled on Chelmsford Street at the back of 7 Westbury Street where his grandmother stands in the late 1920's. Below, George Hall senior in Chelmsford Street with a delivery horse 1930. Opposite a new haulage truck on the same spot in about 1970.

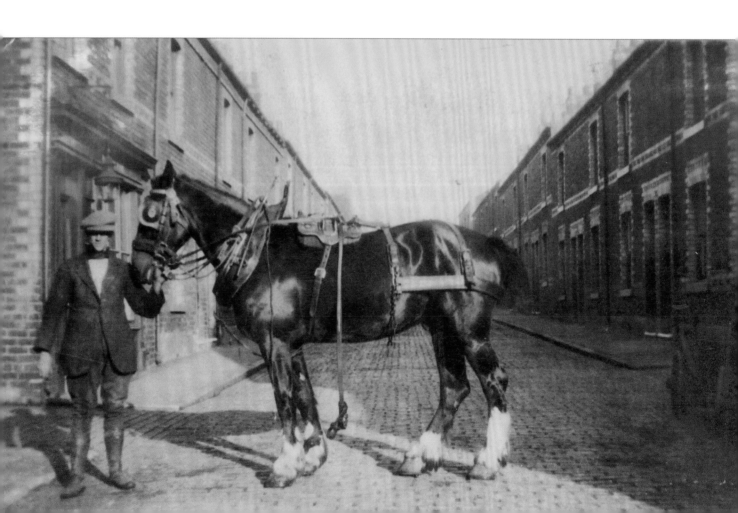

*When my grandfather passed away my grandma was the main one living in Westbury
Street and running the coal side of the business with my father.
She was so generous that she ran the business into real difficult financial problems, if any
body was coming for coal she would take hard luck stories, this was during the depression.
Instead of charging the people for the coal she would give it to them free. So probably
about a third or half of the coal that we'd paid for she was giving away. So the business got
into financial problems. My father then came in to it and sorted the problem out.
All our coal came directly from the collieries at Blackhall, Horden, Easington, Horden,
Fishburn. Every house had a coal fire then but we knew very early on with all the talk about
smokeless zones the general coal business was going to be on it's way out. A lot of the old
houses were going to be demolished the new houses were fitted with central heating. So
we concentrated on the transport side and earlier Dad was going up Brewery Bank from
the gardens where he kept pigs, when a Clevo Flour Mill wagon hit the back of his cart and
he broke his arm. The driver was drunk and Dad got £100 compensation, so he bought his
first waggon, a Dodge from Harewood Garage this was in 1946. There was about 7 or 8
haulage firms in Thornaby so plenty of competition. We had quite a lot of drivers from
Thornaby all top class blokes some of them worked for us for 30, 35 years. We finished up
in the aerodrome eventually when Westbury Street and our house had to be demolished
because of the A66 which went right through Thornaby. They were good little houses.
I was chairman of the road Haulage Association for a while so could see the changes. The
future of our business was so reliant on ICI, we worked for Tarmac as well but then the
whole thing started to change when Tarmac began selling lorries to drivers and they
became self employed.
I'm glad I belonged to an era where running a business was simple. I loved my working
life, but at the latter stages it got complicated. Inspectors from the Ministry could withdraw
your licenses easily for working half an hour longer.
In my early days our driving day was eleven hours now it's eight it shows the big difference,
and we used to work seven days a week, this was legal.*
GEORGE HALL

The Price of Milk

Above, Robinson's Dairies in 1951. The main plant can be seen behind the café which was popular with swimmers from the neighbouring public baths. Jimmy and his father built the dairies on land bought from Lord Harewood for £80, the land that stretched down to the river was offered for an extra £20 but it was declined. Left the Robinson fleet of milk floats and Jimmy in the late 1960's.

There was three farmers in Thornaby delivering milk straight from the cow. At that time in the 1930's there was a lot of people dying from tuberculosis and they blamed unprocessed milk for it. Percy my dad knew all about pasteurising milk. Tuberculosis was killing a lot of people so the government had to do something about it, no doubt about it the milk had a lot to do with it, when it came from the farm it was warm but it should have been cooled straightaway. Father had a machine called a flash pasteuriser, it heated the milk at different temperatures from nought to 150. And then held at that for half an hour and then cooled and so it was pasteurised, we did 1400 to 1600 gallons a day sometimes. We had schools contracts, works contracts, hospitals, we had schools as far as Redcar. Some of the school children were badly nourished, they used to pay a penny for a third pint bottle of milk, it wasn't all free because I remember we used to collect boxes of money with pennies in, after the war it was free.

Our delivery women had to finish at ten in the morning, they'd start very early, six o'clock in the morning do four hours and go home that's what they liked, they didn't want to be working longer. You had a penny profit on a bottle of milk, it was crazy you were fixed by the price you bought the milk at also. You could sell eggs and cream and things like that but it all took time. I think the women got £10 a week in those days doing four hours a day six days a week. They were quite happy it was a good wage in those days.

I managed to get away for a fortnight abroad once a year that was all I could take. I had to be there every day, it was a way of life for me, I enjoyed it. Pals used to say why don't you come and work with us down Head Wrightson's? You'd get more money than working with the father. I liked the business even though it was seven days a week.

The door-to-door delivery declined when they started building modern flats and houses we had all those floats on the road I could see it wasn't going to go, there was no future in it during the 1960s. The new houses had gardens and long paths to walk up, everybody wanted to be set back from the road. When you had the doorsteps on the pavement in a terrace you put the milk on the step and went on to the next one. It took a lot longer to deliver now and then they built these tall flats you had to use lifts, the girls had to walk up the stairs if the lifts were not working.

This girl I got to know she was German, I met her on holiday. I was thinking how am I going to get this young lady from Germany over to live with me and do the business ? So I decided to get rid of the business. Then one day one of the area managers of Northern Dairies came to see me and said we are interested in having a depot in Thornaby, this is ideal for us would you like to sell the business? I thought, God has sent him, it's unbelievable ! Who the hell is going to buy this business and work seven days a week like I've done and struggle like I've done with a fixed margin.

The Northern Dairies didn't see what I saw, I could see it was going to end, there was no future in it. It took another 15 years before they went bang. They paid me an awful lot of money to buy this business, I felt sorry for them. Not long after I brought Helga from Germany and carried her over the threshold. We were 39 years together she was an absolutely fantastic woman, she couldn't speak a word of English at first but I learned the German language and we managed to get through all right but the language of love is a different thing you get through some how.

JIMMY ROBINSON

Ray Garbutt with Peter on Queen Street West 1956, behind,
the Co-op coal depot on Wedgewood Street.

Peter the Horse

*The Co-op coal yard was in Wedgwood Street. From 1954 to 1958 I was working with
Peter on the coal round from Victoria down to Mandale Road and from Thornaby Road
down to Westbury Street. Plus what we called down the steps, Trafalgar Street, Britannia
Street, Chapel Street, that's what I had to do. So that's why I had to work like billyo. I used
to go to the Co-op stables at California Street in Stockton at seven o'clock, Peter was one
of sixty three horses stabled there. The stable lads used to start at three o'clock in the
morning to get the horses out for the milk jobs. When we arrived at seven he'd have
been fed and been groomed, all I had to do was put his tack on take him out and yoke
him onto his cart and then drive to Thornaby. I'd get to Thornaby as quick as possible
and load up with 30 hundredweight of coal in the summer to two ton in the winter
because there was bigger demand. I had to get my work done by half past three because
Peter could tell the time and he wouldn't stand after three thirty. Thornaby town hall clock
used to strike every 15 minutes but once that struck three thirty that was it, he would not
stand that's why I had to work to get everything in. We had an average tonnage of six
tons a day. At three o'clock where ever he was in Thornaby Peter turned around and
made his way to the stables.*

*Every morning he'd get to Mrs Quigley's at Queen Street West and stop and stand there
tapping the kerb with his foot until she came out and gave him a home made scone, or a
biscuit and then off he'd go. When he went across Thornaby Road into Queen Street East
there was a lady there at 29 who used to do the same thing and then off we'd go to
deliver.*

Streets on Peter and Ray's round, taken just before demolition in 1977: above Francis Street, below, Westbury Street and Queen Street.

We got a new transport manager called Ray Pitman, Mr Phillips the retiring manager was showing him round the stable and we were in the tack room, Pitman came in the tack room and looked around, he wasn't at all impressed. He just looked at both sides where horses were and said "These will have to go." and then they started cutting down. So many horses were sold privately, so many horses went to Yarm fair in the October. By 1964 the job was fully mechanized. I drove Peter to Yarm Fair, they put him up for auction I just stood stroking him to say my farewell. When this farmer came along, " I'm having him." and he took him away. "I'm taking him to my farm, but he's going to have a retirement. If you want to come to Harrogate to visit him you're quite welcome" and he gave me his name and his address but I lost it unfortunately and never got to see him from that day. I can honestly admit even though I was in my 20s, I cried like a baby when they took him, I thought the world of him. He was practically human. RAY GARBUTT

The Depot

Thornaby once had the most modern rail facility in the country. Nearly seven hundred people worked at the Motive Power Depot constructed in 1958 as part of British Rail's modernisation programme. Teesside's thriving industry depended on the depot, from here trains moved the products of the oil, steel and chemical industries, coal for the steelworks was picked up from the Durham coalfields and delivered. At Thornaby the locomotives were also stabled and serviced, a vast adjacent freight yard mechanically marshalled the wagons. For many of the workers who had moved to Thornaby from the four "Dickensian" sheds it replaced like

Middlesbrough and Stockton, it was a dream come true. Thornaby meant proper facilities with lockers, showers, the workshops were heated, the pits were illuminated and there was plenty of space within a well laid out site. In addition to the 475 drivers and firemen employed, there were fitters, loco cleaners, coppersmiths, brick arch men, the sheds contained a remarkable range of skills. By 1967 diesel electric had replaced steam trains and staff retrained. Privatisation in 1996 saw all BR's freight depots go over to English Welsh and Scottish Railways. The depot closed in 2007 and demolished soon after.

Left, one of the last steam trains in the octagonal roundhouse,1967. The Roundhouse or Bullring was the centrepiece of the Motive Power Depot with it's 22 lane 70 foot turntable, it was the last steam roundhouse to be built in Europe. The British Rail modernisation programme replaced the old steam trains with diesel, but the roundhouse had been designed with an eye to the approaching diesel technology so it's future was assured. Above English Electric Type 3's (Class 37's) stabled in the roundhouse, 1988.

I began as an engine cleaner in 1957 then promoted to fireman. You know how they say you put the horse to stable it's exactly the same with a locomotive, it was stabled, it was washed, brushed up, cleaned, watered, fed with coal. You'd make sure that the tools were on board the engine, you'd clean the fire out. It was arduous work. A lot of it was shift work, if you started a minute after midnight that was nights. And then you'd have shifts starting at two o Clock in the morning, three o Clock in the morning, four o Clock, eight o Clock in the evening. A lot of us, there's no doubt about it, had problems with our tummies, with ulcers because you were sleeping when you should be eating, you were working when you should be sleeping. The camaraderie was brilliant though, all sorts of characters and some wonderful drivers. I was lucky I was on with a gentleman and once he found out my skills of driving, once he'd seen me operate, we'd go to work half and half. He'd drive one way and I'd drive the other way to give me the experience which was a wonderful thing. We hadn't been there very long, 1966 or so when the diesel locomotives arrived. These were so technical you had to go to school for weeks to learn the ins and outs of the controls of these locomotives. I remember me and my regular driver we both attended this course and on the third day he came out of the class and he said " Oh dear Alan, my head's spinning it's a lot to take in. I tell you what, if we get a diesel on the job it's all yours. I don't want to know I'm retiring in 18 months time. It's going to be your job in the future." 1968 onwards this would be me, I was finally made a driver, something I'd always dreamed of.
ALAN HUITSON

They were advertising for Guards and I fancied being a guard so I got the bus up the old Middlesbrough Road. I said to the conductor " Would you put me off at the Yard Masters?" "I'm awfully sorry you've missed your stop, get off at the next one." He said. So I got off outside the depot and I thought I'll walk in and find my bearings, I walked in and met the time clerk " I've come about this job can you help me?" He said "You don't want to be a guard do you? Come with me." We came outside and there was two brand new class 25 steam trains standing there. He said wouldn't you rather be driving one of them than being a guard?" I said "Of course I would." Come on he said, he took me upstairs and I did a bit of an exam. They took my height and weight and gave me a ticket which I took to Darlington Medical Centre where I had a medical. That was me, fate. If I'd got off the bus at the right bus stop I'd probably have been a guard.

We'd have steam engines bringing steel from Lackenby Steel Works, Dorman Long's Skinningrove then stuff which was for shipment onto the docks. We used to have about six steam engines just shunting at the docks. We ran trains from Boulby Potash. All came through Thornaby, it was a hive of industry. Unfortunately that was the demise of Thornaby sheds when the steel works dropped off because Thornaby was purely freight and the work wasn't there to keep the depot going. JIM SMITH

I thought it was good fun to go to work then but it all got too serious under privatization there was more multi-skilling, they had to make a profit and things seemed to go downhill from there. Especially today the drivers can't turn round today without feeling watched, they have these big black box recorders in the diesels, they monitor everything, with steam you got away with quite a lot. Under privatisation everything became cost, to keep a place like Thornaby running was a challenge, somebody did tell me how much it was costing just for the admin building without the sheds! Then they centralised maintenance and the workshops at Thornaby and loads of skilled people left. To become a manager in charge of train crews you had to come through the grades, you'd have to have been a driver to become a supervisor or train crew manager for example. But in the new regime you could come out of university and have very little knowledge of railways and you could get a manager's position. That was the first stage of it collapsing because most of the people running railways didn't have that background and knowledge. We saw the glory days at Thornaby though, you would never see anything like that again in railway history, certainly not in this country.
RICHARD WATSON

Thornaby fitters replace a diesel engine piston in the straight shed 1988.

Work on an axle, Steve Carr, right 1988.

The roundhouse, right, with the straight shed on the left, this had 11 roads for maintaining engines and carriages, across the Middlesbrough road lies Teesside Park Racecourse. MPD engineer Richard Watson climbed a lighting tower during his lunch break to take this historic 1986 picture, nothing in the foreground scene remains.

Thornaby fitters about 1989 in the straight shed with a model of the Type 60 diesel loco before the real thing came to the Depot, it was one of the most powerful built and essential for moving heavy stock. Many of the 100 made are still in use.

CLASS 60 LOCOMOTIVE
FEATURES

Many of the region's accidents and derailments were fixed by Thornaby's dedicated Tool Van teams. The crew also repaired rail bridges with their 1949 crane. A team at East Cawton in 1988. Bob Willis includes many dramatic examples in his book "Taking the Weight" an account of his life as Thornaby's Tool Van Supervisor.

It was horrendous going in to the straight shed Monday morning especially diesels. there was so many fumes. I can't understand why there was drivers who had failed their medical for say heart problems and they'd be rostered on the shed to start all the class 37's and 47's locomotives. You can imagine the fumes produced in starting them up then running, probably standing all day Sunday if not required and he's a man with a bad heart being taken off as a mainline driver. We started 47's up once and the fire brigade came they thought there was a fire there was so much smoke. RICHARD WATSON

Taken in 1967 during the transition from steam to diesel on the typically busy stretch from the depot and Thornaby station. Left is now Thornaby Place, right George Street and the redeveloped site of the Britannia Hotel which was destroyed in an air raid in 1943 and which also hit these lines.

The Thornaby depot later made a huge contribution to railway heritage. The roundhouse was an ideal facility for restoring condemned steam trains rescued by preservation enthusiasts when diesel was introduced. At least three were completed at Thornaby. The Q6 and J27 engines seen here are still in service at the North York Moors Railway at Grosmont.

PUMPHREY'S
BANQUET
GROUND ALMONDS

Pumphreys

Pumphreys created exemplary working conditions at their Thornaby factories for their mainly female workforce. Run by a Quaker family their works were successful for nearly 80 years producing sugar preserves: jams, lemon curd, icing sugar and cake decorations, building up a worldwide market since 1892. Pumphreys Bridal Icing Sugar and Judge Lemon Curd could be found in kitchens worldwide, Bridal Icing Sugar was also used on a long line of royal wedding and birthday cakes. Pumphreys was one of the first companies to introduce sick pay and holiday pay and regular breaks for their staff, they also encouraged thrift in a savings club with 6% interest.

Left, the entire factory on Archer Street join civic dignitaries to welcome the Czech Ambassador Jan Masaryk in about 1930. Pumphrey's great success in the inter-war years was founded on the imported loaves of high quality sugar beet produced at Malnik in Czechoslovakia. The 1000 ton barges loaded with sugar loaves made their way along the river Elbe to Hamburg for later despatch to the Tees.

Below, Pumphrey's workers and their families gather outside the works entrance possibly for an outing in about 1910. Jim Ashman b.1887 back row far left, has recently joined Pumphreys as a tinsmith working on equipment and packaging, he also designed nozzells for icing sugar flowers. Left, almond processing early 1930's. Jim Ashman on the right, several family members could often be found in Thornaby factories, Cliff Ashman Jim's son was transport manager until the closure.

In 1950 Pumphreys opened an impressive new extension on Mandale Road. The Northern Echo described it as having "A traditional Quaker regard for simplicity and good architecture." The facilities for the workforce was likened to a modern hotel. The new building was equipped with the latest plant machinery for the continuous production of jam, marmalade, fondant, lemon curd.

 On our floor there was long tables, with people making miniature cake decorations out of icing sugar. These were sweet peas, roses, daisies, violets, pansies all made by hand. I went on roses first, Valerie did the sugar flowers, made in two parts and I did the outside petals, We used to do 250 a day. When we did sweet peas she did the bottoms and I did the tops and we did about 3000 a day. Then there was the two Eileens behind us, they did the daisies. On the ground floor there was Mary Quigley and Lilly Frosdick in Preserves where they made raspberry and strawberry jam, it was all done by hand.
My father helped to make a machine to turn the jars and fill them, they were all filled at boiling and it was very clean. Once a year we all used to go down and sort strawberries out, we could eat as many as we liked, but believe me after 7 weeks you never wanted to see another strawberry again.

Mary Quigley on the lemon curd line.

Right, break time photos 1960's including, bottom, sisters Elsie Coleman and Lillian Frosdick.

Packing Bridal Icing Sugar

The atmosphere was absolutely great. We'd send someone out at 10 o'clock for hot pies to Metcalfe's across the road they were lovely. You could talk as long as you got on with your work. Every Monday Jean used to tell us about a picture she'd seen with her boyfriend. We used to put our curlers in, and put our hats over, one good thing about the company hats they covered our curlers so we'd be ready to go dancing at the Maison de Dance that night. JENNIFER GARBUTT (MASON)

The Batty family outside the Prince of Wales in Hope Streeet after refurbishment, 1936. Left to right: Ronald Batty, Sid Haslock, Jack Batty, Berthe Haslock, John Batty.

Batty's

Pub landlords were often celebrities in their own right and became well respected within the community like Jack Batty whose father John gave each of his four sons a pub each to start their married life. Jack was given the Prince of Wales in Hope Street.

My father Sid died at 38, my mother Berthe in 1946 so the pub, Granddad Jack, Uncles and Aunts were a major part of my life for many years. My great grandfather Alderman John Batty was very well known in Stockton, owning several pubs and the Grand Theatre. The name of the pub locally was the Drum and Monkey, but in the early 1930s it was radically rebuilt. I have a very early memory of being bathed in a barrel by a fire before the rebuild. It had a Main Bar, Snug, Smoke Room and Ladies' Room which was mainly for elderly ladies who drank halves. There was also a side door called the jug and bottle where you could take a jug to be filled with beer to take home. In the main bar there were spittoons, a couple by the counter, small ceramic bowls containing sawdust. The floors were scrubbed, and spittoons emptied by Mrs Danks next door and another woman for ten shillings each week. Every day the place was spotless. If there was a wedding reception in the pub, all the young local children gathered outside and sang "throw out your money or you'll have no luck" The men came out

and scattered pennies and halfpennies into the road. A field day for the children. During the war the Prince of Wales became tremendously popular, with all the old customers, wartime industrial workers, and members of the RAF base at Thornaby aerodrome, including Americans. The queues were two to three deep from the end of the road at weekends. Four or five hogsheads were delivered every week . This was the largest of the barrel sizes and held 512 pints each, which gives an idea of the turnover. The delivery of the hogsheads was a fascinating sight. The wagon was pulled by two enormous Clydesdale horses whose hooves clattered on the cobbles. The two draymen were enormous too (or so it seemed to a small girl). with rubber aprons and with huge muscled arms they rolled the barrels from cart to hatch. John and Ronald Batty ran the pub when they returned from the war and their father Jack retired, it continued to be popular until it closed in the 1970's by then the Battys were long gone. RITA BELSON

The Flying Dutchman

Florence and Alfred Dixon

I was 16 when we moved to the pub in about 1949. Dad started off at the Station as a manager then Vaux Breweries did all sorts of alterations and improvements and that's when they changed the name to the Flying Dutchman, then dad became a tenant. We had electricity and we had a bath in the pub we didn't have them before, money was a bit more available. Both mam and dad worked together and it was a lot of work and my dad had a heart attack a few years after they moved in but I had three brothers who did the heavy lifting which helped. It was a very happy pub, we had one or two fights but that was it, mam used to wade right into the middle of it. Our busiest time was on a Sunday lunch time, we used to have a stack of half filled glasses ready for them to come in. It was a large building with six bedrooms and it smelled of hops and polish. We had a big lounge which was mixed and a snug for ladies. Upstairs there was a big room where the RAOB and the Knights of the Golden Horn met. Dad was a member of both of them, like the Mason's they were very secretive. On New Years day, a man hid in the cellar and when the pub closed and everyone went upstairs he came up and robbed the till. When he left through the back door, our dog followed him and later led the police to his house where he was arrested. I had a job there as a barmaid when I was 18. I remember the horses that came with the drays they were impressive. It wasn't easy running a pub, when you closed on a night you weren't finished, you had to do your cleaning up and get ready for the next day. I was married from there in 1952 and my husband and I used to look after the pub when mam and dad went away, then we were offered a pub of our own but we turned it down, it was too tying, my mother and father were so fortunate in having three sons and two daughters to help out. The chap who had it before them was a prisoner of war in Japan George Leverette, he'd been on that notorious march, his feet were terrible. Then after mam and dad the manager from The Bradford Vaults came to run it. He'd been a deep sea diver and had a brass diving suit on display, they were the last people in there. It's a tragedy that a magnificent building like that should disappear. JOAN RETALLICK

Scholastic Souvenirs

Extracts from an album of Queen Street school photographs from the early 1950's taken by the Scholastic Souvenir Company who began photographing schools in 1911 and who are still in business. The school population had increased by two million, while post war austerity and major cuts to the education budget by the 1951 Conservative Government must have left their mark on Queen Street, a board School opened in 1884. Yet in spite of limited resources the dedication of the staff is evident. The work of the 1944 coalition Education Act and implemented by the Atlee Government raised the school leaving age from 14 to 15. It also meant free school meals for low income families at last and thanks to the efforts of Ellen Wilkinson, free school milk to all children. There had been an acute wartime shortage of teachers and Queen Street, but mainly the secondary schools, would benefit from the Emergency Training Scheme for teachers to cope with the extra pupils. Many ex-servicemen and women were given grants to train as teachers on a year's crash course. The controversial 11- plus exam was also introduced.

Above: George Snow takes a class for a BBC Schools Broadcast, below, blinds are drawn for a lesson with a film strip projector which is plugged into the light socket above.

Alec Crawford teacher, John West, Geoff Wilson, George Warboys, Ken Close, Ralph Frazer, Keith Wilson, John Norman. 3rd Row: Ian Hendry, Peter Voules, Hedly Drake, Keith Moore, Eric Scott, Norman Bradley, Gerald Glasper, Jefffrey King, Noel Salmon, Tony Wright, Ali Mohammed. 2nd Row: Keith Warriner, John Otterson, ? Bridgewater, Colin O Brian, Colin Notman, Stanley Burnett, John Wrigglesworth, Eric Robson, Norman Sutcliffe, Cedric Colins, Malclom Maleary, John Cook. Front Row: Raymond Warboys, Harry Andrews, Barry Hetherington, Raymond Pinnegar, Jimmy Race, Eric Whitfield, Charles Barton, Allan John, John King.

That's me front row third from the right, I remember doing some of those drawings on the wall in the background, we split up into groups: the Saxons, Normans, Romans and Vikings, you were in that group and you did the research and read up about the history and made drawings of how they lived, what the transportation was like and so on. Mr. Crawford came to work on his bike from Stockton, I remember in one class he put it upside down on the desk and we had to draw it. Later on he drew a straight line on the blackboard with a large ruler and for some reason I laughed out and Crawford brought me to the front of the class and caned me. He taught every subject, you stayed with him for the whole year, they were general teachers. You had to knuckle down a bit because you had to sit the 11 plus.
ERIC WHITFIELD

The 1944 policy required schools to provide nutritionally balanced meals and free to children in low income households. In 1954, school dinners were off site in this prefab hut behind the Baptist Church on Thorntree Road. Queen Street installed kitchens and dedicated eating areas a few years later.

Netball group near the King Street entrance to the school, about 1964.

I think this photograph must have been taken in 1964 because Elaine Speight is still there on the far right and she left in third year, emigrating to Australia. I remember the Pop music of the time especially the Beatles and Tom Jones. My dad first rented a TV in 1961 so we saw it all on TV: there was Ready Steady Go and later Top of the Pops. The buildings in the background of the photograph look drab but we didn't know anything else in those days, it was home. Fashions were changing and you no longer had to wear what your mother wore. I was the only girl in the family so I did have some new things but one or two hand me downs as well. There wasn't a lot of money around and for some families it was all hand me downs. In the early 60's, everyone seemed to be very prim and proper, the girls had those full skirts and little white ankle socks and all the female teachers carried handbags on their arms. Everyone dressed formally with most of the boys in a shirt and tie. As we got to 1966, things were a lot less formal, everybody was more individual in their dressing style and there was a sense of fashion.

We all look quite healthy in this photograph. We had the NHS of course and I remember going down to the Welfare for inoculation against the main diseases and we had dental check-ups as well. Most of us look quite well-nourished. We had so much freedom as kids especially with there being so few cars on the road. We also had the Littleboy Park and Victoria Recreation Ground (the Rec) in which to play. You talk about being healthy, we were out playing all the time, skipping and playing ball games. When Wimbledon or cricket test matches were on TV, we had the tennis rackets and cricket bats out.

Our 11 Plus exam success was all down to Mrs Degan. She had a reputation as a dragon with a deep, husky voice. We were all scared as anything going into that fourth year. Mrs Degan really did push us, having tests every week. I remember her husband wore a bowler hat and often brought her to school in an old Rolls Royce. There were 44 pupils in our class and 22 of us passed the 11 Plus so it was an exceptional year, all down to Mrs Degan, she was a great teacher. Looking back, it seems so wrong that young children should have been segregated in this way. I did a secretarial course after grammar school. I do regret not going to university but when our daughter was doing her A levels, I studied for a social sciences degree at the Open University as a mature student. By the time I'd graduated, she had her first degree and was working; she is now practicing as a GP. The school had a strong work ethic, which influenced me and perhaps I've passed some of that on. MARGARET BOWEN (HIGGIN)

Queen Street staff in 1966. Mollie Degan third from left, back row. Next to her, George Snow. Headmaster Brian Moores is front, third from right, Charles Harker second left, and Donald Sinclair, Alec Crawford, second right, then Betty Peverill.
Possibly taken at the end of school year when Mollie Degan gifted a book to each of her 44 departing pupils.

Mollie Degan's production of Dr Who 1966. Dr Who was played by Carol Huitson (Parker), Susan, Joyce Leeson, Stephen, John Greenley. The Daleks included Helen Cartwright, William Robinson and Lesley Huckle. Photograph taken by Headmaster Brian Moores, a keen photographer whose films of the school can now be viewed on Youtube. Pupils benefitted from the many extra mural activities Mr Moores encouraged and helped to organise.

I passed the first half of the 11 plus in about 1956 but must have been borderline since I had an interview at the High School and didn't get in. There was no grammar school in Thornaby so they allocated places for Middlesbrough High School and Yarm Grammar. But we had so few places, some years out of all the Thornaby primary schools there might be only four places allocated. It shows how comparatively deprived Thornaby was where so few children reached Grammar school. I lost my father at 11, he was being treated in hospital at Newcastle and we moved to Sunderland for four months to stay with my mother's sister. The class was taking it's 11 plus, I'd taken mine already and nearly all the A Class passed the scholarship. The teacher said "If you'd been here you'd be on your way to the Grammar school." PAT MCSORLEY

A Sharing Society

During Thornaby's industrial heyday residents found most of their shopping needs in the town and no where was busier than the Co op or the Stores as it came to be known. The Co operative Wholesale Society formed in 1863 emerged from the hardships of industrial life, where access to quality goods was costly and ran along the principles of ethical trading and sharing of profits. Thornaby residents who became members collected their dividend or divi at the end of each year according to the amount spent. The Stores provided nearly everything a person needed from the cradle to the grave.

"The Stores" on the corner of George Street and Francis Street near derelict before demolition in 1977 to make way for the A66 carriageway, and the scene now. As Thornaby expanded in the 1870's so did the demand for provisions and the Co op opened Number 1 branch in 1876. In addition to provisions and clothing a large social room (left corner first floor) provided space for dances and meetings, it was hugely popular. The site was a hive of activity.

I started in 1962, I left school on the Friday and started work on the Monday.
It took me 2 minutes to get there and 2 minutes to get back to 21 Francis Street where I lived.   We were opposite the labour Hall, I remember Jeremy Bray the MP when he got elected, there was dancing in the streets. The drapery part went round from Francis Street to George Street, it had a shoe department and a gents outfitters, the general drapery was downstairs. Next door there was the grocery, then a tobacconist, a chemist and round the corner the greengrocers and butchers. The department started to contract in the 60's, you could get measured for a suit but it was made up in Wellington Street in Stockton. The wages were decent, I earned £3/5/11 weekly.
We had lots of sales which I enjoyed because then the days just flew by. After I got married and later had my baby I went back afterwards, unfortunately I contracted glandular fever

and I was in hospital. I was handing sick notes in to the manger and she said "Oh don't bother they never ask for them." So I stopped handing them in, then a girl came to the door with my cards.

I loved serving people and replenishing stock, writing the dividend numbers out in the checkbook, you'd write how much the customer had spent and tore it off and gave it to the customer with the dividend number, that's how they got their dividends. At the end of the financial year they'd count how much everybody spent and that's how you got your money back. I loved working with the people there, we all got on. I used to dress the windows as well, you had to change the displays every two weeks. I loved the Christmas window, it was amazing setting out all the gifts, we had very good sales on aprons, the men used to come in on Christmas Eve and buy their wives aprons for Xmas, very imaginative. BARBARA GRIMES

I started at 14 in Havelock Street Co op during the war and finished at 22. We had a butcher, greengrocer and general provisions. I cycled far out to get customer's orders, I used to go as far as Thornaby Green, then the orders would be delivered. Nothing was packed, we had to pack and weigh everything up ourselves. You had a big wooden container with stock in and one of us would stand filling the bags, another one weighed them, another did the wrapping, another at the other side put the items in the fixtures. In those boxes there was everything- we weighed up sugar, soap powder, soap flakes even pepper. Biscuits came in big boxes you had to transfer them to paper bags.

Havelock Street hadn't any refrigeration in those days, the sides of bacon used to have cotton wrappings and they'd hang in the cellar. The cellar was open at one end with wooden crates where the cheese stood, big round cheeses. There was a wire with wooden handles and you'd have to pull this through the cheese to cut off a circle and that went up to the shop where it was cut into pieces for sale. I was taught how to bone bacon and take out ham bones, all the machinery was mechanical. Butter, lard, everything came in barrels so you had to cut it and weigh it. You had the chits to write out for the dividend. When you did the selling you'd put the cash in a container and pull the handle and it went up to the cashier in the office by wires and pulley. The wall had an opening in it and you could see the cashier's face.

When I started on the bread counter there used to be a queue right round waiting to buy the fresh bread. I moved from there to the bacon counter then on to groceries. It was wartime rationing and we sometimes found with big families there was so much they didn't buy so they'd barter with others. You weren't stuck to one particular job if they were short on the grocery counter "Would you go up there Edith ?" And you'd help out.

On my co op deliveries there was a bungalow right up Thornaby Road opposite the airfield and he was head of the Emporium in Stockton. They had a fashion centre there and he used to look after the fashion parades and one day he must have been in when I called to do the ordering and we got on talking and apparently later on he'd got on to my manager at Havelock Street and he wanted to transfer me to Stockton to model in his fashion parade and I found out later from his wife that my manager wouldn't let me go.

EDITH WHITFIELD

Edith first left front row with staff of Havelock Street Co-op in about 1946. Taken at the side of the Registrar's building opposite. The site today on the corner of Peel Street and Havelock Street.

Council cleaning operatives at the back of Wellington Street 1976, right, Leslie Stone.

Margaret Hope
Easter, 1959
photographed by
Judy Heslop

On Grange Road

I took this photograph of Margaret Hope when she was about nine. The films only took eight photos and were quite expensive at the time. I think I only ever had two films. I also had a flash attachment. My uncle Bob Huggins showed me how to develop them but we never had the money to go on with this as a hobby. Grange Road was a lovely street to live in then.We used to play in St Paul's churchyard the door ways of the art Deco Mayfair cinema and the cornfield opposite. We were just across from Thornaby baths. After swimming we'd go to Robinson's Dairy cafe for Oxo and crisps. My husband and I bought our first home there in 1969 for £800 my parents had paid £800 for theirs in 1946, there was no inflation in those days. JUDY HESLOP (HUGGINS)

My Easter dress was bought from Doggarts in Stockton High Street, it was pink with rose buds. The camera was a gift from my gran who won it in a Whist drive. When we took the photographs there was only two or three cars in the road including my dad's sister who was a midwife in Newcastle. I had to be sparing with the film because it was expensive and used up all my pocket money with five of us in the family there wasn't much money. I can't remember what happened to the camera but dad took up photography later on and joined a camera club. MARGARET HOPE (GRIFFITHS)

Golab Singh on his wedding day with Grange Road neighbour in 1976.

My father passed away in 1968 he had a heart attack while on a ship in Hartlepool as a ships chandler. He was only 36 and there was nine of us so we all had to support my mam who came to Thornaby in 1970. Some of the communities living in Middlesbrough at that time came to Thornaby where the property was better value. We couldn't legally buy a house because none of us was 18 at the time even if we had saved the money but when my brothers became 18 they were able to buy a house in Cambridge Road. They were top houses at that time, we thought they were for the relatively well off and we knew they were well built. We all left school at 16 and began work, I was an apprentice plater and served my time for eight years, my brother was a plumber, my eldest brother was a mechanic another worked at British Steel in Cargo Fleet. Jobs were easier to come by at that time than what they are now, we all seemed to have a job there was Head Wrightson then. We helped our mother and each other. In our tradition we were responsible for our sister's weddings so we had to marry them which was an expensive sort of thing but we all stuck together, there was a lot of unity. There was a strong community in Thornaby at that time, you could walk into anyone's house, the keys were in the door, money was on the top of the milk bottles. The neighbours were very welcoming. I started off here making fireplaces down by the Bon Lea, then next door to Ken Jacksons, making trailers. We mixed pretty well, for example a lot of the Seikhs gathered at the Roundel and played darts, we even won a charity tournament in 1972. I never encountered any discrimination in Thornaby, I was just brought up with everyone else, there was never any hatred. My grandfather was one of the first Seikhs to settle in the area in 1936. There's always been a merchant talent in the family he was a peddler and my father was a ship's chandler. The new generation is for education, everyone is trying to get a degree, accountancy and pharmacy are popular with the family today. GOLAB SINGH

Social Housing

Thornaby Council was very successful in building and managing subsidised housing in spite of the post war challenges which were enormous with a council waiting list of 1460 to fulfil. No projects had been completed during the war and many homes had been damaged or destroyed. A major problem was finding land for building on and it wasn't until the airfield site became available in 1962 that the problem was finally solved. Belvedere Road was a small development built on farm land off Diamond Road and is typical of the style of housing the council adopted at the time, these were quality homes for social renting. The Council had a Direct Labour force of nearly a hundred building operatives based in Sun Street for maintenance, and construction. Estates like the Littleboy, Cornfield and Holmes Close were all built by teams from Sun Street. "The Yard" was also a valuable source of apprenticeships and skills. Belvedere, possibly because of yard capacity at the time was built by a private Thornaby contractor Coultas and Shaw. On later completion of the New Town on the airfield the majority of homes in Thornaby would be social housing, until well into the 1990's rents and homes remain affordable.

Belvedere Road under construction 1954 by Coultas and Shaw Limited. Second from right is Alf Bayles, next left Denis O' Riordan.

David Allport and his family were some of the first residents of Belvedere Road in 1955, his experience is common to many who moved to new council homes from the terraces of the old town with no facilities.

Left: ice cream outside 15 Belvedere Road, from far right: Mrs Allport with David, Mildred Hall, far left Carol Hall, Joyce Allport, on step Marlene Gibson taken about 1956.
Right, spacious, safe streets for play, David and Joyce Allport with friend.

We'd moved from Mann Street in 1955 with no facilities, to our new council house at 16 Belvedere. My parents thought it was heaven, for the first time we had a bathroom and indoor toilet, two fires and a back boiler. Many people wanted gardens and we finally had two, one front and one back. Uncle Eddie my mother's brother who lived with us was a great gardener, he loved growing things, we always had vegetables. Behind our house was Mandale farm where they still had livestock, it was just over our garden fence, it was just like being out on the edge of the country.

There were so many young people our age in the streets to play with and lifelong friendships formed. This is Billy Gibson and me on our trikes. Billy became the best man at my wedding and I was the best man at his. DAVID ALLPORT

A New Town

Mayor and Mayoress John and Dorothy White with council officials survey the plans for the new Thornaby at the town hall 1963.

A bold vision to create a modern town with every facility became a reality when the RAF vacated the airfield site in 1957 but it then took several years of negotiation with the Air Ministry to purchase the 347 acres before the dreams of the Thornaby councillors could begin to be realised in 1962. Although smaller post war estates such as Littleboy and Mandale were gradually completed, a rising population and the decaying Victorian slums of the original industrial community placed constant pressure on housing waiting lists. Not only would quality low density social housing be now provided in the council plans but all the elements that helped a community thrive, the shops, schools, churches, leisure, sports and health centres were here. On the perimeter a 300 acre industrial estate would provide some of the new jobs. 150 acres was dedicated to private development. The planners adopted the recently published and highly influential Parker Morris report which recommended a range of new standards of living in homes, from space and heating to children's play areas. It was also believed that residents were willing and now able to pay for these higher standards. By 1968, 1000 council houses had been built and occupied with a further 189 under construction of 900 planned. Consequently the focus of Thornaby shifted from the old industrial town to the airfield. No separate New Town authority was created to execute and supervise the project which was handled entirely by the Town Council. For a relatively small Borough like Thornaby this was a notable achievement.

Demolition of slum properties: Railway Street and right, a rare view from Thornaby Place towards the Bridge Hotel

Seen on this and neighbouring pages are frames from 8mm films shot by Les Watson, Thornaby Borough's Engineering Surveyor and Planning Officer for 22 years. He was closely associated with all phases of the development and praised by architects and civil engineers for his work on the project. Les filmed all stages of the development from it's inception, thankfully his family preserved these valuable reels of film after he died in 1991, they show us in detail the creation of a new town.

My mam and dad helped me get a trade on the council through Edna Huck the councillor, she got me an interview with Bill Powers and an apprenticeship in the summer of 1962, I signed my indentures at the Town Hall. We mainly did maintenance to the council properties. Then they sold the airfield and after that they were building all over, there was any amount of contracts and I went on my own after serving my time at the council. I enjoyed the trade and by then I could build houses from the foundations up including electrics, plumbing, plastering, the lot, I had the knowledge and skills. I went to the Abbey National and they wouldn't give us a mortgage, they said You're a casual worker. You mean I can build houses but I can't buy one? Yes. He said. That's it. But you couldn't fall off for work especially in Thornaby. The vast majority of it was social housing, council houses. What caused the problem later was Mrs Thatcher selling the Council houses, the private sector moved in and they started putting the rents up because they could. When I was first married we lived in Shackleton Court where we were paying £2.75 a week, then it was only a small proportion of my wages of say £20 a week, now it could be a third of it at least. I go past jobs I did years ago and say "I built that." It gives me satisfaction. KEN PAYNE

Right: Lingdale and Staindale Roads from Hudson House 1965.

Mayor James Kidd presents keys to the first resident of Hudson House 1966.

Sir John Wrightson unveils "Thornaby" the sculpture by Brian Wall outside Wrightson House in 1968. The piece had been fabricated at Head Wrightson Teesdale works and was believed to be the largest metal sculpture then made in the UK.

Crowds of spectators in St. Peter's Square at the Town Centre opening in May 1967.

Officials view the James Kidd footbridge

Anthony Wedgewood Benn Minister of Technology opens the Town Centre May 12th 1967

I was a joiner, there had been a severe winter of 1963 and we had all been out of work, no one could do any work for 3-4 months because of the snow and the conditions. You'd be queuing up to sign on twice a week at the Labour Exchange on Bridge Road in a foot of snow and they'd ask you " Have you been looking for work " You must be joking, if you can get me a job in all this I'll go. If you didn't sign on you'd get no benefit. I had two kids then and we got £5.19.6 week. So the aerodrome housing was a godsend because there was so much work. Even guys from places like Loftus came down because there was no work up there. There'd be a squad of four of us with a labourer, we did a lot of roofs, a lot of it was bonus work. The quicker you did the job the more you made as a bonus. The managers would come down and give you a price for each house, you might get 25 hours to do a house. If you did it in 20 you got 5 hours bonus which would often be £5, so it was a great incentive. You didn't stop long for any dinner and tea! You just went at it all day. There was no electricity on the job, we just had oil lamps in the winter, if you were walking round the site you took your lamp with you. The houses were open shells, it was very cold in winter. There was no real protection only your boots, gloves and overalls. Toilets were two oil drums in a metal hut with a round seat on the top and that was it. All the roofs were timber, the trusses and rafters were all cut by hand on the floor with a big circular saw. There was no crane, the brickies had a hoist but most items were manhandled up with a pulley and a rope. After the first fix and the roofers did the lead flashing the electricians and plasterers moved in then we went in to mark out the joists and lay the floor boards in each room before finishing off with the door frames, doors and kitchens. The clerk of works came round to check everything and pass the work once you got in to it you knew what he wanted. Some of the joiners were getting top money, because there was so much going on, you could finish one job and go to another contractor down the road where the bonus was better. I visited the Dales estate years later and it was still in good nick, I felt a real sense of pride "I helped build that." DAVID GREEN

In 1967 we left Cuthbert Street to go to Kilbride Close, believe it or not Cuthbert Street had only been connected to electricity in 1962. You know the Clampetts in the TV series "The Beverley Hillbillies" well our move reminded me of them. Me dad worked on the council then and he used to have a wagon for the lighting so he used that to move us, I sat on the back of it, we hardly had any furniture. There was seven of us altogether, I can't describe what it was like walking in and seeing a fitted kitchen and a bathroom upstairs, it was like winning the pools, and we couldn't believe it just to walk in the garden with the sun on your face rather than a back yard. It was like a new world, they were good quality houses as well. We had a garden at the front and a garden at the back so we could put some veg in. JOE DUNN

We got this house in Hamden Way in 1973 the lady over the road here lived next door to us in Denmark Street where we came from which wasn't very nice with a private landlord and he hadn't done much with the repairs. They automatically re-housed us in a council house because the old terraces were coming down. It was heaven, the first thing I did before we even moved in was have a bath because we had an actual bathroom. My husband used to carry a tin bath from my mother's in Francis Street to our house in Denmark Street on his head to have a bath, luckily we had an Ascot boiler, we had hot water and we didn't have to boil kettles like many people did. It was absolute luxury up here to have an inside toilet - two in fact and a bathroom. Some of the people we knew from the old streets were re-housed here with us. Then they built the town centre and it was brilliant because everything was up here now. There was loads of families and the kids played out together for hours on end in the spaces, growing up round here was perfect for my children. BARBARA GRIMES

Above Jack Marwood and the resident band at the Maison de Danse, Stockton the popular dance band active until the late 1950's. Popular music was soon to undergo a radical change.

The Bands

The Milestones at the back of 7 Poplar Road in 1963, Ken Payne on drums, on the table is Kenny Kitchen with Dave Neal in donkey jacket. John Nimmo far left.

What changed everything was Pop music. Everyone was singing Beatles songs even the old people knew about them. Things got brighter, fashions were more popular, there was more money about, more people were working and they began to have a different attitude and started to smarten themselves up. I was in the Milestone's for a while as a drummer. Life on the road may sound romantic but it was demanding. All we had was one amplifier, an American valve amplifier you could hardly lift it up. Everything was live then we had no backing tracks to support us. Del and the Falcons used to rehearse in a house on Thornaby Green, we used to sit on a bench outside and listen to them, to learn how to play well. KEN PAYNE

It is 1962, the Rolling Stones make their debut at the Marquee club and the Beatles arrive from Liverpool to record their first single, *Love Me Do,"* For many young Thornaby people the early 1960's was something of a revolution after years of austerity and 1950's drabness and popular music was at the heart of the changes. Through juke boxes, radio stations like Luxembourg and vinyl records a new world was emerging in the town and the clubs and pubs throbbed with live music created by local bands. Thornaby boasted seven decent bands at one time in the 1960's.

Del and the Falcons at the Maison de Danse 1965 Mervyn Jones, Malcolm Willis, Pete Embleton, Paul Butler.

Del and the Falcons

The Oddfellows Arms was our first gig and soon after we were booked most nights. What blows us away is how many consecutive bookings we had. We'd be home at two o' clock in the morning then get up and go to work, it was an astonishing pace of life. We had something our parents didn't have which was the freedom. At fifteen, sixteen we were out playing until the silly hours, and we were given that trust by our parents. We were not conscious of it being revolutionary which it was. The Oddfellows was our first gig, we were only 15. In this area the Working Men's clubs were the social scene. You'd do the first hour and you couldn't get anyone's attention. They'd have their bingo, the pies were cooked then you'd go back on at 8.30 and by 10 o'clock they wouldn't let you off! Some of the other venues were death traps though, they were in basements, a bit like the Cavern . But the atmosphere you generated in these places was remarkable. The time was just right for bands, you started off innocently, we got £4 cash for that Oddies gig and we said thank you very much, we all had our little day jobs, but we did it for love because you

enjoyed the playing, you enjoyed the adoration, it was great.
We were so fortunate to get it in at the right time and be competent enough to be good and also be appreciated, to have a good run before it all changed. We burned ourselves out though when you look at the bookings diary.

Del and the Falcons at Elmwood Youth Club.

In the beginning: Mervyn Jones' garden on Thornaby Green. Left to right, Mervyn, Paul Butler, Paul Clasper at the back, Malcolm Willis, Pete Embleton,1964.

We once supported Freddie Star and the Flamingoes and he borrowed our Fender Stratocaster guitar. This was the fun we were having, there was also camaraderie with other bands , a little bit of competitiveness only to be better. Some bands sounded good because they had good gear. Often you'd be doing gigs with other bands you'd do two gigs together and it would be great afterwards because and you'd ask " Where did you get that song from " Same with professional bands. We supported Wayne Fontana who had just recorded "Game of Love." At the end of that night they taught us a song that hadn't even come out. We tried to remember as much as possible the following day when we met up. We'd buy two singles on a Saturday morning, whatever was new in the charts then we'd learn it Saturday afternoon and we played it Saturday night. Some band members went on to be professionals but as we progressed with our work careers and marriage the excitement of the decade began to fade. Also competing trends were just around the corner. The Discotheques destroyed everything, they took music away from musicians, this was the beginning of the end. Things have to change and by the end of the 60's it seems people had had enough of live music and the DT's took over. MALCOLM WILLIS AND PAUL BUTLER

I was Perry and the Victor's drummer. At first I didn't have a car or transport, we didn't have a group van so we relied on friends to take us. One Sunday we played a date at Seaton, there was me and one other member, we made a dash for the last bus to the clock tower

to get to the Transporter and we missed it. So there's me and him walking along the Tees Road at midnight and it threw it down. All our kit had gone ahead in a car, that's why we couldn't get a lift, the cars were full of all the gear. I still had all my band gear on and I was soaked. And this was all for about £15 between five of us. No one ever moaned in Raisdale Crescent where I lived on the Dales estate when I practiced on my drums, we also had a session at my house and all the kids in the street were outside listening. ERIC WHITFIELD

Eric Whitfield on drums with Perry and the Victors 1965

Johnny Rocco, second from left with the Rock Avons 1964

Ronnie was a moulder at Crosthwaites foundry during the day but by night he had his white suit and became the singer Johnny Rocco. I met him at the Sadler's Hotel when he sang the songs that were popular at the time, Cliff Richard, Billy Fury and Elvis Presley, this was pre-Beatles they hadn't come on the scene yet. There was a lot of pubs with entertainment going on, the Sadlers, the Windmill. The Windmill had a jukebox where we all used to meet, there was the Bon Lea as well. Ron worked with a number of bands as their vocalist but could gig on his own as well, so he was always in demand. As Ronnie got older he did more clubs, by the 1970's a lot of the bands split up and went their own way and they got married. Then Ronnie started to do the clubs. He also did alright on New Faces and Opportunity Knocks. He could have been professional but as soon as we got married and we had Dawn and Dean he wouldn't do it, he'd had offers to go back touring again but he wouldn't leave the children. Johnny Rocco did well locally as a vocalist for nearly 30 years moving from band to band and sang into the 1990's.
MAUREEN PORTER

Johnny Rocco, sings with the Midnighters, Grangetown Magnet Club 1965

Firefighters

Until 1971 Thornaby was a retained – a part time fire station. There was quiet a complement of firefighters and some great people when I first went down. Now young un Now Young un that's all I got when I went down. I didn't realise most of them were either ex Navy or Army and doing the job some from the 1940's. Their knowledge was unbelievable. The first day I went on a chimney fire, Jimmy Speight shouted "Just make sure you put it down the right chimney." On part time you have your day job, when the sirens go you have a bell in the house and whole time is you work a shift system which then was 56 hours. Your night shift began at five o clock at night to nine o clock next morning which is 16 hour night shifts and you were totally destroyed if you had a busy time. Sundays if I was on duty my dad used to bring my dinner down, it was a brilliant place. I was already heavy goods I had my HGV 1 but you had to a test, I could drive the engine but had to be trained over six months, it was a different thing ten ton of machinery doing 60 miles an hour you had to have your wits about you. The new tenders had high capacity hoses and if you went into a house fire you could rapidly reduce the temperature in the house by using one of these high capacity hose reels, this formed a mist which interfered with the molecules of the gasses of the fire. If you went in to a house fire you would see dragons it was unbelievable, it was just like a dragon coming towards you. It's not a magic thing to put a fire out, it's where you aim your hose, that's how you knock the fire out.

In the early days we talked amongst ourselves to cope with trauma. I could cope with it to a degree, some lads didn't like it at all, they just couldn't cope with it, but in the early days it was just get on with it. We'd come back and talk about it talk about the incident, could we do it better ? This was early 1980's. Eventually we got an occupational health nurse and if anybody wanted help they were there. You could see people wanted help. In the early days away you went, I think it was a lot to do with the age group, colleagues in their fifties, army and navy veterans who'd experienced warfare and they just accepted it and this was just passed on to you. It is much better now, but you need support when people lose lives, it's awful and horrible, it does affect you. If you talk about it even next day it will gradually disappear. The camaraderie was amazing, a laugh a minute and I don't know where the 30 years went from day one. I dropped money to go to the fire brigade it was dedication, even when I came out as an officer the money was rubbish really, it's starting to creep up now. As an emergency service considering the tasks that we did , it was underpaid, especially for putting your life on the line. Mrs Thatcher she got us the money, she got us our 48 hour week, she looked after us. The 56 hours was a killer, it was a rolling programme whether it was holidays or not, trying to get Xmas off, no chance, your name was put in a little hat and if there was one spare you could have it. Other stations were in the same predicament.
RAY TWEDDELL

Top right, Thornaby Fire Brigade in 1962. Front Row left to right, Mr. Greenwood, Ernie Retallick, Jimmy Speight, F.Roberts, Jack Beadnall, J.Harper. Back Row left to right, A. Wheelhouse, T. Alderson, Dennis O Riordan, George Frosdick, Nancy Hugill, Mr..Alderson, Joe Haydon, E.Peacock, Billy Gale. Bottom right, the fire station in George Street about 1971 before it changed from a retained to a full time station.

Dr Stephen with staff, Thornaby Health Centre Surgery 1990's

On Call

My brother was a GP in Redcar from the mid 1950's, I was up and down and I knew what the area was like, so I came here to work, I liked the area. I hadn't any previous experience of an industrial area where I was born in Montrose in Scotland where my father was a GP pre- NHS days.

A lot of people worked in awful conditions here, there was also a lot of pollution, a lot of asthma, emphysema, chronic chest complaints. I can't say there was more than in other areas but more than say in a rural area. There was more smoking and beer drinking then. In Thornaby many people worked in the steelworks and heavy industry and they also tended to replace their fluids with beer. We had quite a few patients who were heavy beer drinkers. I can't imagine it's the same now.

We would be 5 or 6 partners at the practice so we shared the emergency duty between us, anything that happened, anything that came in was dealt with by one doctor. You could be going to somebody who'd just had a stroke and you'd get a call to somebody else who'd had a heart attack. Which one do you go to ? There was a lot of stress, the doctors certainly had a lot on. There certainly wasn't the emergency service back up at that time. Because there were times when you were so tired. I can remember one Saturday night fortunately and I was out during the night for eight calls. The next day was Sunday but it could have been Monday and it could have been a normal day seeing 50, 60 people. There was more availability of beds then than there seems to be now, they were busy then but you could always get a patient in if they had something serious.

I was the first to have a mobile phone that would be 1994. Before that I can remember going around maybe on a Sunday doing calls and the only way to check up on developing calls was to go to a telephone box and phone our call taker Mrs Mason to see what was in. I had to find a phone box that worked and you could go to three different phones in the centre of Thornaby and none of them worked, they'd all been vandalised and then you'd have to go back to the Health Centre. I maybe worried about it more than others, I was always anxious that something could be happening and I was out of touch and I got more anxious until I found a phone. I was always very conscious of being on call and how important it was. DR GEORGE STEPHEN

Dibbles Bridge, Grassington, North Yorkshire, May 1975

Dibbles Bridge
Britain's worst road disaster.

On 27th May 1975 at about 15.30 a coach of 45 female senior citizens from the Thornaby area crashed into Dibbles Bridge at Hebden in the Yorkshire Dales, ploughing through the bridge parapet and landing upside down in the garden of the cottage below. 32 people were killed including Roger Marriott the driver and 14 seriously injured, one person died in hospital a month later. The tragedy remains Britain's worst road disaster and still stirs strong emotions in the town today where only recently plans for a proper memorial have been drawn up after over 40 years. As he lay dying Roger Marriott was able to speak to a passing motorist and whisper to her that his brakes had failed. Later an extensive study of the wrecked coach revealed a faulty brake lining, although a combination of other factors such as the steepness of the hill, and lack of warning that the bus was approaching a notorious accident black spot contributed to the disaster.

JRH 758E in Sheffield the year before the crash. Riley's bought the Bedford Duple from a company in Hull in 1974, it had been new in 1967. The bus left the home of operator Norman Riley at 22 Stranton Street at 9am on the day.

I can remember looking through the front windscreen and thinking this bus is going awfully fast something is going to happen and it did. It was a bit like being on a roller coaster. The next thing I remember was seeing a fireman looking through the window of the bus and saying close your eyes we're going to get you out the next thing I knew I was out on the bank of the river and then being carried to an ambulance.
MARGARET ROBINSON

The bus came to rest in the garden of Dibbles Bridge Cottage, by this time the injured had been taken to Airedale General Hospital near Keighley.

News of the disaster reached the front pages of all the national newspapers the next day.

The movement of a bus made me feel sick so I used always to get in the front seat to look out then I wasn't sick. That day I had to go all the way to the back because the front seat was taken by the organisers. They said " You'll be alright on the back seat. " And as it turned out it was. We had all been looking forward to the trip. We got to the steep hill and the bus went over the top to go down again and all at once it picked up speed and that was it. I came round, then I was off again, when I came to I was in hospital and Barbara and the family were round the bed.
MAY RICHARDSON

We were going up this hill and the lady came round with raffle tickets for a disabled boy we were supporting. We got to the top of the hill and I looked and thought what a lovely view, I turned to my friends and they were asleep and as I looked over I saw all this black smoke coming up the side of the bus. And the next thing I knew I heard the sound of rushing wind, it was terrible and then I heard the sound of breaking glass and then I heard no more. And then I heard " Wait a minute there's one here " then I must have been in hospital and the next thing I knew I woke up in bed. The sound of wind and breaking glass was terrible, I can still hear it. DOREEN PARKINSON

Councillor John White and Dorothy White greet visitors to Thornaby Council chamber in 1962.

Below, the dancing Class, 1950's

Trip organiser Dorothy White served as Lady Mayoress in 1962-3 and was once described as " The Good Samaritan of Thornaby" Renowned for bringing people together in the town Dorothy was also active in the Women's Royal Voluntary Service and Townswomen's Guild. The trips Dorothy arranged for senior citizens were complemented by two play groups and popular dancing classes for young people. Left, an earlier trip to the coast.

A view from the opposite bank of the crash site shows the natural beauty of the location but also reveals the difficulty of access for the emergency services. The winch truck parked on the bridge ordered by PC Metcalfe helped to raise the back of the bus sufficiently to free one person but the process was stopped due to fear of the coach chassis slipping.

Ena Hill, right, with her friend Ida Fisher on an earlier trip to Fountain's Abbey

The next thing I knew I was at my sister's house and a news flash came up about the accident in the Dales and I just knew straight away. I said to my sister "Grandmas on that coach." She got a little bit upset with me because she said "Don't be silly." I ran all the way from my sister's to my mam's and when I got to our house I could hear my mam crying so I knew she'd been on there but it was quite a while before we knew she'd died. CINDY DAVIES granddaughter of Ena Hill.

We are talking from a 21st century perspective when all the service has specialist rescue equipment. They were using hand tools to free people from inside this coach, they were using hacksaws to cut through seat frames, they were unbolting seats to make access easier and it was a long and slow process. BRIAN DOOKS Journalist

We were in the hospital waiting for news and I said I'll just go and get a coffee and I went to this area and there was lots of people and I realised they were pals from school, people I knew from the streets and I asked one young guy who I knew how was his mum ? He said his mum had died but there was a woman in intensive care and everyone was clinging to the hope that that lady, just maybe was there mum. CAROL VON VANKARTHY

PC Jim Metcalfe's incident sheets. Jim recognised the importance of the documents and copied them, they have become a unique piece of history since the originals were destroyed.

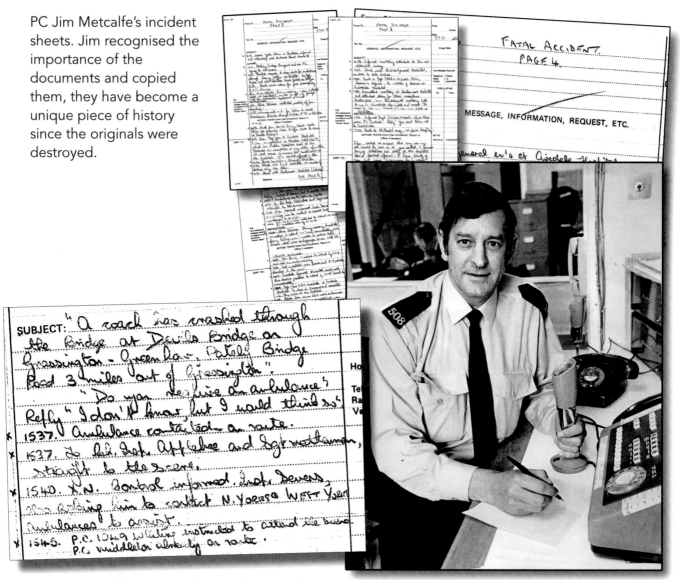

PC Jim Metcalfe was on duty at Skipton Police station on the day of the crash, he took the first call at 15.37 and remained continuously on duty until 21.30. Jim dealt with the emergency single handed since civilian staff were on holiday. Despite moves to replace him Police HQ decided his local knowledge was essential to dealing with the emergency.

Lincoln Seligman, the first person at the scene was holidaying with his partner at Dibble's Bridge Cottage which belonged to his father in law. Lincoln saw the bus after it landed in their garden yards from the kitchen where they were preparing a barbeque. He stayed to help until the last victims were removed from the scene. At the end of the work Lincoln moved to a hotel in nearby Pateley Bridge for the night before leaving for London. He never returned to the once popular Dibbles Bridge Cottage which the family later sold.

Local farmer Basil Cardus took his powerful tractor with equipment to the crash scene and volunteered to help raise the coach chassis but police and firemen feared it might cause more damage to those trapped inside. Basil's father attended the 1925 crash, memory of the scene caused him to have nightmares over the next three months.

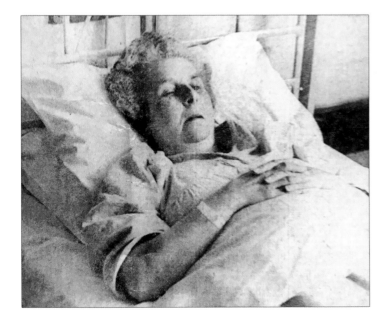

The three youths who were first on the scene at the Hebden coach disaster, Carl Dickinson, 16, Stephen Jennison, 19, and Stephen Griffin, 15. (A Yorkshire Post picture.)

Three teenage campers from Hull cooking in their tent in the next field heard the screech of the handbrake. Stephen Griffin stood up and witnessed the bus ploughing through the parapet and land below. All three spent the next three hours working at the scene. Stephen Jennison, Stephen Griffin and Carl Dickinson were reunited in 2018 for the documentary filming.

Survivor Mary Booth of Humber Road. The newly opened Airedale hospital was well placed to take the casualties. Many nurses and some of the doctors lived in on site accommodation, the response team was assembled in 20 minutes and they were ready to deal with the first arrivals.

Dibbles Bridge - a terrible legacy

1924 A motor lorry crashed through the bridge parapet and onto the bed of the stream below. No casualties are recorded.

1925 A charabanc carrying York Municipal Officers on their annual outing crashed through the parapet, somersaulted and fell below when the brakes failed. Seven were killed and 14 injured one person died later. The inquest recommended widening the bridge and the road. Neither are carried out.

1933 Two men injured on a club outing when a motor coach with brake trouble carrying 30 passengers escaped disaster knocking down the bridge wall but remained on the road.

1969 A truckload of sheet metal from South Bank lands by the stream, the driver jumps out in time and survives.

1975 A coach of 45 mainly senior citizens from Thornaby crashes through parapet after brake failure and somersaults onto the garden below in exactly the same position as the 1925 disaster. 32 are killed including the driver and one person dies later, there are 14 serious injuries.

1988 A truck carrying a load of pine roof trusses crashes through the parapet somersaults and lands below.

2014 32 years old cyclist James Nelson from Skipton fails to return home from an evening training ride, his body is found next to the stream the next morning after going over the parapet.

2015 Doctor George Ballard, a cardiologist from Ilkley and a keen cyclist is killed after hitting the bridge on August 2nd after losing control and somersaulting into the stream below.

2016 North Yorkshire County Council carry out a feasibility study resulting in metal grills being attached to the parapet mainly for the protection of cyclists.

Above left, Dr George Ballard, Dibbles Bridge from the stream, right, James Nelson.

Photograph taken by Jonathan Longthorne shows the truck carrying pine roof trusses which crashed in 1988. Jonathan's grandfather was born in Dibbles Bridge Cottage and witnessed the 1925 crash.

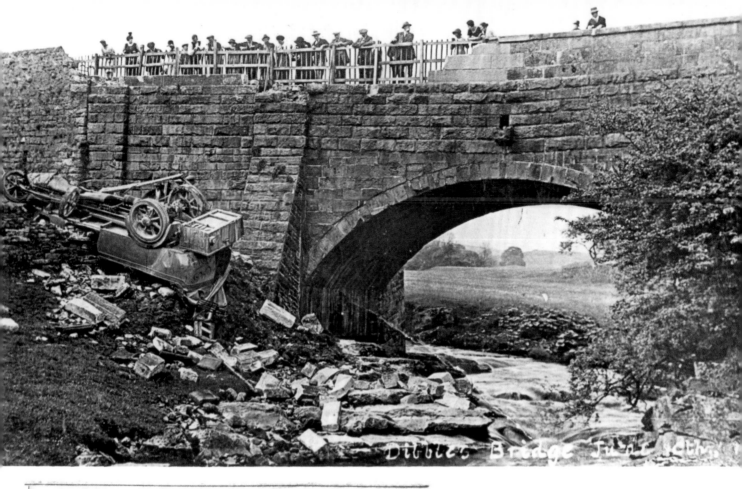

Dibbles Bridge July 16th

Miraculous escape of lorry driver at Dibbles Bridge

In uncannily similar circumstances to the 1975 tragedy a charabanc crashed through the parapet in August 1925 after the brakes failed. The charabanc was taking York Municipal Officers on their annual outing. Seven were killed and 14 injured, one to die later. The inquest recommended widening the bridge and the road. The road authorities were blamed for not implementing the recommendations of the 1924 accident.

Ken Rogers of Ormesby jumped from this truck of steel plates from South Bank on 1st August 1969 before it ploughed through the bridge parapet and onto the ground below. Mr Rogers was assisted by Ken Longthorne a local haulier and later admitted to hospital in Keighley for severe shock but made a full recovery.

Doris Howsden

Gwendolyn Dodsworth

Ena Hill

Hettie Kirk

Roger and Joan Marriott

Mabel Chisholm

Dorothy White

Gladys Callaghan
and Joan Hymer

Kathleen Maud

May Richardson

Rosaline Brown

Eva Rodgers

Edna Dobson   Lillian McLeod   Jennie Lowe   Harriet Riley

The Injured

Alice Benson	Edna Dobson	Joan Marriott	Madeleine Pratt
Mary Booth	Joan Hymer	Doreen Parkinson	May Richardson
Edna Clemenson	Lillian McLeod	Helena Pickering	Margaret Robinson
		Eva Rodgers	

Those Who Died

Betty Aitchison	Gwen Dodsworth	Doris Howsden	Harriet Riley
Margaret Baldwin	Ida Fisher	Henrietta Kirk	Eileen Ross
Lillian Barclay	Hannah Forth	Jenny Lowe	Jean Smart
Rosaline Brown	Hilda Gibbon	Roger Marriott	Eva Thomas
Jenny Butler	Irene Groskop	Kathleen Maud	Dorothy White
Gladys Callaghan	Grace Harrison	Margaret Mennell	Freda Wilkinson
Isobel Chisholm	Edna Heron	Elsie Middleton	Edith Woodhouse
Ada Christon	Elizabeth Hill	Henrietta Pedley	Sylvia Worn
		Eva Pratt	

Doreen Parkinson   Edith Woodhouse   Hannah Forth and Jenny Butler

End of an Age

By 1980 when this photograph was taken the focus of the town has long shifted to the airfield and to the emerging Ingleby Barwick development. When Head Wrightson closed in 1984 so did the main source of work and especially apprenticeships in the town for over a century. Landmarks like the Queens cinema and the railway station are demolished, many of the popular pubs and clubs, once cornerstones of industrial community life also disappear. Thornaby lost it's independence as a municipal borough and as a town in 1968 when it was absorbed by the new county of Teesside which later became Cleveland County in 1974.

Some residents speak of a loss of identity and an inability to influence major decisions as a result of being part of a larger authority. Like minded groups soon formed though to re-affirm the town's status and they were effective. The Remembering Thornaby Group for example successfully campaigned to have the Town Hall listed, they also gather oral history, and intervene when the rail authority plan to change the rail station's name to Stockton South. Then in 1995 a Town Council is created within Stockton Borough Council even though based in Yorkshire. By 2003 a full scale renaissance is under way spearheaded by Thornaby Town Council who oversee the Town Centre redevelopment and along with many other initiatives begin to publish a quality magazine showcasing activities within the town, it restores confidence and pride. Symbolic items like the Mayoral chains are finally returned from storage in Stockton, the rescue of the decaying town hall becomes a cause célèbre.

The A66 dual carriageway had a dramatic effect on parts of Thornaby, splitting the old industrial community in two as it ploughed through a ladder of streets, shops and pubs. Above, waste land where Durham Street once stood, 1977, Queen Street School, left, through the gap. Left, the Queens Cinema in 1976.

Margaret Thatcher's 1987 "Walk in the Wilderness" on the derelict Head Wrightson site at Teesdale symbolised for many the passing of the industrial age, not only for Thornaby but the whole country. Once 2000 people worked here, now Thornaby and Teesside are unemployment blackspots with nearly 20% unemployment as steel, shipbuilding and engineering decline. At great public cost The Teesside Development Corporation regenerate the Teesdale site and promise: "The Venice of the North East." A Business Park, Durham University Campus and College of further education are created along with housing developments such as Victoria Quay. Mrs Thatcher returned with Sir John Major ten years later to highlight the transformation during their unsuccessful 1997 Conservative Election campaign.

A 1988 panorama, Teesdale is cleared and returns to it's almost virgin state of two centuries ago to prepare for regeneration. There are no signs or markers in the new development to acknowledge the industry that was based here and it's contribution to the national and local economy over 100 years.

POSTSCRIPT: Thornaby Town Hall

This is the best example of Victorian architecture left in the town and still functions as a civic building, however nearly 15 years of dereliction and neglect left it's mark. Stockton Borough Council, custodians of the town hall failed to replace stolen lead from the roof during the 1990's and for many years thousands of gallons of water poured into the building. The ingress destroyed whole sections of the original moulded plasterwork across all floors and also caused structural damage. It was feared for a while that the Town Hall might be beyond repair and have to be demolished. Thornaby Town Hall narrowly missed being sold by SBC to a private developer who demanded the eviction of Thornaby Town Council as part of the deal. TTC challenged this in court and won.

In 2015 Thornaby Council prepared and was awarded a Heritage Lottery Grant for funds to restore the building to it's original splendour and function as a working building once more. Thanks to the struggles of TTC Thornaby Town Hall has been brought back into the ownership of the community it was built for: it is now owned by the people of the town and set to become a community hub once more.

Some of the restoration team: top, Michael Atkinson architect with site manager Trevor Gamble. Left top and bottom John Powson, Ryedale Plasterers releases a new panel from a silicon mould. Left, on the stairs from right, Les Roberts, Steve Gamble, Neil Brindly, Kevin Gamble, Ben Golden.

THE AUTHOUR

Born in Barnard Street where he is seen here on the far left in 1958, filmmaker and photographer Derek Smith has won many awards for his documentary films. His documentary about the Dibbles Bridge disaster also commissioned by Thornaby Town Council, is being screened on television throughout 2020 and 2021.

ACKNOWLEDGEMENTS

Thanks to our archive sources:

Remembering Thornaby Group Archive
John Watton
Thornaby Public Library
Middlesbrough Local Studies Library
Laura Gibson, Picture Stockton
Stockton Library, Local Studies staff.
Kimberley Starkie and staff,
Teesside Archives
Chris Lloyd, The Northern Echo
Christine Hutchinson
and Christopher Young
Preston Park Museum.

The Imperial War Museum
Mary Evans Picture Library
Ann Dixon, Gazette Media
Armstrong Railway Photographic Trust
North Yorkshire Police
Scholastic Souvenir Co.Ltd, Blackpool
Special Collections,
Leeds University Library
Darlington Railway Museum, Alison Grange
Historic Environment Scotland.
Yorkshire Post Newspapers

A grateful thanks to:

Pat Allison
Richard Barber
Tony Bartley
Stuart Bell
Alan Betteney
Marjorie Braithwaite
Rona Bromley
Myra Brook
Maurice Burns
Ann Burns
Basil Cardus
Steve Carr
Bruce Coleman
Robin Cook
Sandra Costello
Elizabeth Cousins
Martha Davies
Al Davies
Cindy Davies
Eileen Dobson

Stephen Dobson
Mickey Dodsworth
Christine Elliot
Mark Fairbairn
Louise Faragher
Ian Ferguson
Chris Fernihough
Gillian Frosdick
Mia Klokkers
Sylvia Hall
Neil Hampton
John Harding
Doug Hauxwell
Keith Heslop
Nick Hill
Ken Hoggett
John Howsden
Peter Hymer
Michael Hymer
Stan Laundon

Ken Longthorne
Stephen Longthorne
John Lowe
Ethel Lowther
Ian Macdonald
Alison Madden
Sandra Main
Frank Mallon
Doreen Malone
Jennie Maud
Amanda McLeod
Jim Metcalfe
Philip Moore
Stephen Moon
Brian Nichols
Ken Pettit
Dean Porter
Emma Parker
Ann Peterson
Ellen Nelson
Maureen Reed

Trisha Reece
Barbara Reeve
Denis Rigg
Dave Robson
Albert Roxborough
Anthony Sheldon
Eunice Spence
Joanne Swansborough
Pat Swift
Norman Toulson
Ethel Tyreman
Carol van Vadkerthy
Vanessa Wass
Bernadine Walker
Richard Watson
Christopher White
David White
Lesley Wickens
Craig Willis
Bob Willis
Malcolm Willis

A special thanks to our interviewees:

Kathleen Alder
David Allport
Rita Belson
Margaret Bowen
Paul Butler
Peter Clark
Alan Clark
Fred Costello
Ken Craggs
Yvonne Crone
Cindy Davies
Joe Dunn
John Eccles
Dougie Fairbairn
Harry Foster
Raymond Fulton
Howard Fulton
Norman Fulton

Ray Garbutt
Jennifer Garbutt
Gladys Godwin
Henry Godwin
David Green
Jack Green
Barbara Grimes
George Hall
Cath Harrison
Douglas Hauxwell
Eileen Henderson
Judy Heslop
Fred Hicks
Margaret Hope
Mary Hudson
Alan Huitson
Mervyn Jones

Don Lackenby
Catherine Luck
Christine Lymer
Matthew Marley
Pat Macsorley
Winnie McHugh
Ken Morrison
Clifford Morrison
Vincent Paleschi
Doreen Parkinson
Ken Payne
Bill Pickering
Maureen Porter
Barry Preece
Joan Retallick
May Richardson
Margaret Robinson
Jimmy Robinson

Jim Smith
Eric Spavin
Dr. George Steven
Pat Stokes
Beryl Story
Enid Thurlwell
Dorothy Toulson
Ray Tweddell
Ethel Tyreman
Connie Wass
Richard Watson
Edith Whitfield
Eric Whitfield
Malcolm Willis
Linda Wilson
Anne Wilson
Maynard Wilson